047448

LEARNING RESOURCE

S0-EBT-510

HQ   Moses, Alice E.
75.5
.M67   Identity management
1978   in Lesbian women

DATE DUE		
RECEIVED NOV 1 7 1995		
APR 2 5 1994		
FEB 0 7 1995		
NOV 3 0 1995		
RECEIVED MAR 2 7 1996		
APR 1 4 1996		
2 0 APR 2000		
0 8 DEC 2000		

mill Woods

© THE BAKER & TAYLOR CO

IDENTITY MANAGEMENT IN LESBIAN WOMEN

Mill woods

HQ
75.5
'M67
1978

IDENTITY
MANAGEMENT
IN LESBIAN WOMEN

Alice E. Moses

Foreword by
Eileen D. Gambrill

LEARNING RESOURCE
CENTRE
GRANT MacEWAN
COMMUNITY COLLEGE

PRAEGER PUBLISHERS
Praeger Special Studies

New York   •   London   •   Sydney   •   Toronto

Library of Congress Cataloging in Publication Data

Moses, Alice E
    Identity management in Lesbian women.

    Bibliography: p.
    1. Lesbianism. I. Title.
HQ75.5.M67 1978   301.41'57   78-23742

PRAEGER PUBLISHERS
PRAEGER SPECIAL STUDIES
383 Madison Avenue, New York, N.Y. 10017, U.S.A.

Published in the United States of America in 1978
by Praeger Publishers,
A Division of Holt, Rinehart and Winston, CBS, Inc.

89   038   987654321

© 1978 by Praeger Publishers

All rights reserved

Printed in the United States of America

This book is dedicated to my Father,

Harold R. Moses

and to the memory of my Mother,

Elfin Genevra Delano Moses

FOREWORD

Eileen D. Gambrill

Until recent times, homosexuality has been viewed within the
helping professions and by people at large as distinctly negative. It
is still viewed as such by many people. This conceptualization was
strengthened by the growth of the mental health movement with its
tendency to view deviations from the norm as a sign of pathology.
This view of homosexuality encouraged studies designed to root out
the causes of this atypical behavior that would hopefully shed some
light on how to readjust homosexuals to the mainstream of society.
The focus was on describing the pathological aspects of homosexuality.
Over the past years, this model has received vigorous competition
from other frameworks that differ in critical ways from a negative
view of homosexuality. These newer frameworks of labeling theory
and social learning theory do not have a vested interest in finding
pathology. Labeling theory focuses upon the very process of labeling
itself. Rather than taking a label for granted, labeling is viewed as
a process of social definition that may or may not be accepted by the
person so labeled. How does someone get to be labeled as a homosexual or to so label himself or herself? And what are the effects
of this labeling process? Here was a radically different perspective
from the medical view of homosexuality. Rather than focusing on
the individual per se, there was an enormous widening of perspective
in terms of the events examined to understand the process of labeling,
and the social context within which this occurs. This theory empha-
sized the relativity of labels and the influence of labeling itself upon
maintenance of a deviant career. There was no assumption that homosexuality or anything else for that matter, was pathological. The
fact that the American Psychiatric Association recently removed
homosexuality from their list of mental disorders reflects the con-
sensual nature of such definitions.

The importance given to social interaction within labeling theory
compliments that within a social learning perspective in which one's
social relationships with others are viewed as critically important
in affecting his or her behavior. As in labeling theory, there is no
view of a given behavior as being pathological per se. In both, there
is a focus upon the interaction between behavior and the social context within which the behavior develops, is maintained, and changes.
In both, there is a recognition of the social definition of behavior and
of the process of social interaction related to this and also of the
influence of different situational contexts. In the older perspective,
one is or is not a homosexual; like one has or does not have TB.

Being freed from a view of homosexuality as pathological broadened potential areas for investigation in another important way; one could and should examine all consequences of a deviant label; that is, there might be beneficial consequences as well as negative ones. To find these, it would be necessary to gather descriptive information concerning relevant behaviors as well as information concerning the surrounding context in which these behaviors occurred. Thus, another important way in which these frameworks differed from the older perspective was in encouraging a finer grained analysis of behavior in its situational context. There was a far greater appreciation of the complexity of everyday life and of the way in which interactions affected the labeling process and the behaviors labeled.

Being freed from a pathological focus also generated different questions, such as the one raised in the study reported in this volume. How does one manage a deviant identity? The report is not addressed to the question: how does one get along in the world with a handicap? Posing questions in this more neutral stance leaves one more open to finding continuities between the experiences of all individuals, whether labeled as deviant or not, as is discussed by the author. Since we all apply certain labels to ourselves and since we all engage in identity management behaviors at one time or another, this study like others of its type, offers a more unified framework for viewing behavior. Abnormal and normal behavior are considered to be influenced by the same variables, although how these may be played out in each individual's life may differ vastly.

An important advantage of the newer framework for viewing deviance, is the fact that the data generated offer more information to direct intervention when concerns arise. This report presents descriptive information concerning how a sample of lesbian women manage day to day interactions with others. What behaviors, if any, are avoided and what behaviors, if any, are performed concerning identity management? This volume also explores the relationship of selected factors such as visibility, to management behaviors. Identifying specific areas of concern for a selected population and identifying what is done in these situations are important first steps in the development of intervention programs that will be relevant to a population. This is the first study that offers information concerning what women actually do or do not do in order to pass and describes some factors related to the ease of management. This report is an excellent illustration of the complimentary nature of labeling and social learning theories. One useful direction for further research would be the even more refined identification of relevant behaviors in specific situations. It is also an excellent example of the use of quantitative and qualitative data. In addition to testing out selected hypotheses in relation to variables associated with identity management, a rich variety of qualitative data is offered concerning, for example, what being a lesbian means to this sample of women, including positive aspects as well as negative aspects. The further exploration of positive aspects of an identity as a lesbian woman is another area for further research efforts.

I think the reader is likely to be well rewarded from a careful reading of this book. The introductory chapters contain excellent descriptions of labeling theory and of conceptualizations of identity management. The author shows appreciation for the complexity of the process of identity management and makes excellent use of available literature in describing this concept. The data presented is an addition to the sociology of deviance and should be helpful to professionals who work with lesbian clients. The author is sensitive to the changing position of homosexual people in our society in terms of the growing gay rights movement and the greater readiness of many homosexuals to make themselves known. Sample limitations are recognized and discussed.

Is being a lesbian a handicap over which lesbian women consider they have little choice or is it a positive choice on their part that is very satisfying? Are there frequent management problems? How do lesbian women manage visibility issues? And how much does thinking about being identified influence risk taking behaviors? How are the concerns of living life as a lesbian woman viewed in relation to a possible choice to live as a heterosexual woman? The reader may be in for some surprises concerning the data presented, which relate to these questions.

ACKNOWLEDGMENTS

This study was undertaken as part of the requirements for a doctorate taken at the University of California, Berkeley, in 1977. Its completion and publication represent the combined efforts of a number of people. While it isn't possible to thank each one individually, the author would like to express a most heartfelt thanks to all of those whose time, energy, and support made it possible.

The author would also like to offer special individual thanks to the following:

First, those women who were willing to take the time to complete the questionnaire and thus provided the data on which this study is based. Perhaps as much as for their help, I'm grateful for what they taught me about the strength, courage, and joy that are to be found in the lesbian community.

Dr. Eileen Gambrill who chaired the dissertation committee and who, more than any other individual, provided guidance, support, and reinforcement; who was always available when needed and is an exceptionally fine teacher.

Drs. Arlene Hochschild and Leonard Miller for their input and support as members of the dissertation committee.

The administration, faculty, and staff of the University of Tennessee School of Social Work, Knoxville Branch; especially Professor Norma Taylor and Dr. Nancy Lohmann (now at West Virginia University, Morgantown) for keeping me going, Dr. Roger Nooe for much-needed administrative support, and Ms. Kathy Rauch for being generally remarkable.

My parents, without whom there would have been nothing, and especially my Father, who wanted a daughter more than a son and told me so.

Audrey Putnam to whom my debt of gratitude is beyond words.

And last but not least, the women of High House who thought that the whole thing was a good idea even when I wasn't too sure and provided nourishment for the soul and subjects for the research.

CONTENTS

LIST OF TABLES

INTRODUCTION

Until the 1970s, the majority of "scholarly" literature on lesbians and lesbianism, sparse though it was, was written from a psychoanalytic point of view (for example, Bieber 1962; Bergler 1957; Caprio 1954; Deutsch 1933; Freud 1924; Kaye, et al 1967; Keiser and Schaffer 1949; Wilbur 1965). Beginning in the 1960s and increasing in the 1970s, a number of studies, articles, and books have appeared which view lesbianism and homosexuality from a non-pathological viewpoint (for example, Abbott and Love 1972; Cory 1965; Gagnon and Simon 1973a; Goode and Troiden 1974; Johnston 1973; McCaghy and Skipper 1973; Martin and Lyon 1972; Plummer 1975; Simon and Gagnon 1967a, 1967b, 1967c; Ward and Kassebaum 1964; Weinberg 1973; Wysor 1974).

Much of the writing on lesbianism, whatever its theoretical approach, focuses either on the sexual behaviors of lesbian women or on describing lesbians and the lesbian life style. With some anecdotal exceptions (for example, Abbott and Love 1972; Cory 1965; Galana and Covina 1977; Martin and Lyon 1972) surprisingly little has been written about the ways in which lesbian women manage their lives as simultaneous members of lesbian and straight communities. Little is known about the ways in which lesbian women function within the straight community, what makes such functioning possible, and what makes it easy or difficult to manage.

Contrary to popular stereotype, lesbian women are frequently not identifiable as such (Goode and Troiden 1974; Martin and Lyon 1972). Because of this, it is possible for lesbians to move back and forth between the lesbian and straight communities, engaging in behaviors appropriate to each. Such women may simultaneously lead lives of apparent outward conformity to societal norms while in the presence of nonlesbians and nonhomosexuals (that is, "straights"), while having private lives which would be defined as deviant by the conforming majority. There are at present no data which delineate the actual behaviors engaged in or avoided in various situations by lesbian women, or which identify the factors involved in such management. This study is an attempt to do both.

Although lesbianism will be referred to throughout this book as socially deviant behavior, it must be stressed that the author does not believe that there is anything inherently deviant, pathological, immoral, destructive, or dysfunctional about lesbianism as a sexual preference. It is believed that lesbianism is a viable, if sometimes difficult, life style. It is not believed that lesbianism leads to, or is symptomatic of, pathology, neuroses, dysfunction, abnormality, or perversion. The words "deviant," "deviance," and other synonymous or related terms used in this study to refer to lesbians and lesbianism are meant to reflect the attitudes of society toward lesbian women as these are manifested in laws, moral and religious codes, psychological and psychiatric diagnoses and treatment, and most importantly, in the reactions of heterosexual individuals (Goode and Troiden 1974; Kitsuse 1962; Plummer 1975; Simmons 1969). At least as far as personality variables are concerned, there are to the author's knowledge no studies extant which demonstrate pathology or dysfunction on the part of lesbian women when compared with non-lesbian women. What few studies exist seem to demonstrate the reverse, if anything (Armon 1960; Gonsiorek 1977; Hopkins 1969; Siegelman 1972; Simon and Gagnon 1967c; Thompson, McCandless, and Strickland 1971; Wilson and Green 1971).

The primary framework to be utilized in this study is that of labeling theory. Labeling theory is considered particularly appropriate because of its attention to the societal reaction to deviance and the effect of this reaction on the deviant. Individuals within the labeling perspective have examined the process of becoming deviant as well as the reality of being deviant (for example, Becker 1973; Goffman 1963; Lemert 1972; Matza 1969). Within this perspective, deviance can be seen as a process, perhaps even a negotiation of sorts, between the deviating individual and those members of society with whom (s)he comes in contact. This view of deviance is directly relevant to the substance of this study.

An overview will be given of deviance theory, with particular attention to labeling theory and identity management. Labeling theory will then be related to lesbianism with the resultant formulation and presentation of the major hypotheses tested.

IDENTITY MANAGEMENT IN LESBIAN WOMEN

1

DEVIANCE

Deviance theory has grown out of both criminological and sociological theory. Until the mid-1930s, the prevailing view of deviant phenomina was a correctional one, with researchers and theorists at pains to discover the causes of deviant behaviors and thence to do away with them and with deviants. Theory and research concentrated on criminal behavior and on the criminals themselves (Matza 1969; Taylor, Walton, and Young 1973). In the 1930s, however, a new attitude toward deviance and deviants began to develop which Matza (1969) terms "appreciation." In contrast to the correctional attitude toward deviance, the appreciative sociologist is apt to empathize with and attempt to understand the people and phenomena (s)he is studying. Concurrent with this appreciation of the deviant, the assumption developed that deviance is a natural consequent of laws, codes, and expectations and, thus, is as inevitable and perhaps unremarkable a part of social life as is conformity (Becker 1963; Erikson 1962; Scheff 1964).

In the area of sexual deviance and abnormality, there are other theorists who, following a social learning model, have questioned the notion of psychopathology and have begun to ask how individuals learn any kind of behavior, not just behavior which is considered socially deviant (Gagnon and Simon 1973a; Ullman and Krasner 1975). Both the sociologists and psychologists who have taken these later approaches focus attention on the function of social labels in definitions of pathology and in determining the reactions of others to an individual who is labeled as deviant.

LABELING THEORY

According to Lemert (1972, p. 14), the proponents of labeling theory are "distinguished by the importance they assign to symbolic interaction and social control in the understanding and analysis of deviance." From the labeling perspective, deviance is seen as a matter of social definition, rather than as something inherent in a given act.

> Deviance in this view is a social construction and takes on variant meanings according to the situation and the individuals interacting. It is not something well defined upon which most members may agree; rather, it is something fragile which has to be negotiated. Every social situation is bounded by implicit rules that differ greatly from the 'formal' rules that sociologists traditionally have studied, and whenever such rules are violated . . . deviancy definitions become a strong possibility (Plummer 1975, p. 24).

The definition of deviancy to which Plummer refers frequently involves the application of a label. When this occurs, there can be a host of consequences (Becker 1973; Erikson 1968; Goffman 1963; Kitsuse 1962; Scheff 1964). Whether the label in question is assigned actively by society as in the case of the senior citizen or the alcoholic at an AA meeting, or self-assigned by the individual, the consequences can be the same (Plummer 1975).

Lemert (1972) points out quite accurately that the consequences of being labeled are not necessarily complicating, unpleasant, or undesirable, although frequently they are so. While a label may provoke social sanctions and/or personal discomfort, it may also provide the individual with entry into desired circumstances or escape from undesired ones. For example, while the label "lesbian" may cause an individual to be considered or to consider herself as sick, such a label may also provide the individual with contact and entry into the lesbian community and may provide her with an exit from undesired heterosexual relationships.

The manner in which a particular label and its implications and consequences is handled depends in large part on two factors: the visibility of the deviance for which the label is assigned and/or assumed and the primacy or importance of the deviance for the individual and for others. Labeling theorists generally distinguish between two types or degrees of deviance based on an individual's commitment to or involvement in a deviant life style: primary deviance and secondary deviance (Lemert 1972).

Primary and Secondary Deviance

Primary Deviance

Lemert (1972, p. 62) defines primary deviance as the original deviant act which, "while it may be socially recognized and even defined as undesirable . . . has only marginal implications for the status and psychic structure of the person concerned." As long as the primary deviation is not completely unacceptable in the context in which it occurs, it may be dealt with as being within the boundaries of normal social behavior, that is, be normalized. The boundaries of the existing rules for acceptable behavior are stretched or altered to include the deviant behavior (Goffman 1963). For example, the man who gets drunk at the annual office party and makes a fool of himself may be excused because, after all, it's only once a year. The ground rules of propriety are stretched to make allowance for the behavior without classifying the offender as a drunk and without punitive or corrective measures of any great severity. Note that if the same man were to do something more extreme while under the influence of alcohol, for example, make a pass at the wrong person or become involved in a drunk driving incident, the individual's status might indeed change, and severe negative sanctions might be applied along with a label. He would no longer be someone who just gets drunk once a year, but someone who commits unacceptable, dangerous, and perhaps punishable offenses. The consequences of this second type of label might be more severe. If a label (for example, drunk driver) or an official punishment is given, the individual may be on the way to becoming a secondary deviant as will be explained below. In general, however, an individual with otherwise impeccable credentials as a nondeviant (that is, one who is by definition normal) may be allowed to act in ways which might be considered suspect and unacceptable for someone without those credentials. Even in the event that a severe infraction occurs, the individual's previously clean slate may hold the labeling process off, as in the case of the individual who is arrested and then released on his/her own recognizance.

Secondary Deviance

When the deviance in question is considered socially unacceptable and therefore is not normalized, it is likely that society will resort to "stigmatization, punishments, segregation, and social control" (Lemert 1972, p. 63). The deviant is labeled. Under such circumstances, the deviant individual may undergo or perhaps undertake a change in self-image such that the fact of deviance becomes an integral part of the definition of the self. Following such a change in self-definition, or concurrent with it, may come a change in life style in order to successfully incorporate the consequences of the particular type of deviance. Some examples of this might be the involvement of the drug addict in the drug culture to the exclusion of all else; the management necessary for the prostitute, homosexual, or ex-convict in attempting to belong to a deviant social group while interacting with straight society; and so forth. The effects of deviant status on the deviant have been described in detail elsewhere (Becker 1963; Erikson 1968; Goffman 1963).

Rubington and Weinberg (1968) assert that for successful labeling to occur, all parties involved must agree on the new definition of the individual. Critics of labeling theory have based their arguments in part, however, on the fact that deviance sometimes occurs without labeling having taken place from outside the individual at all. These critics suggest that labeling theory casts the blame for deviance primarily on society and on agencies of control without taking account of the fact that sometimes these agencies are not involved in the creation of the deviant individual (Akers 1968; Mankoff 1971; Taylor, Walton and Young 1973). Plummer (1975, p. 21) points out, however, that

> it is not an argument of interactionism that specific
> people actually have to react towards a deviant for
> 'labeling' to be successful: it is often sufficient for
> the individual to simply react towards himself. 'Self-
> indication' and 'self-reaction,' then, may be just as
> analytically important as societal reactions. Thus,
> for example, a person who experiences homosexual
> feelings does not have to be hounded out of town, sent
> to prison, or treated by a psychiatrist to come to see
> himself as a homosexual—he may quite simply 'indicate'
> to himself, through the 'interpretation' of the given
> feeling and the accompanying awareness of the societal
> hostility, that he is a homosexual.

Thus, it seems likely that for successful labeling to occur, the individual really need only be aware that a particular type of behavior is one which is viewed by society as deviant and that there are consequences for that type of behavior which may be applied to the individual if the deviance becomes manifest to nondeviant others. As long as the individual is aware that society (1) reacts in certain ways toward those who are lesbian (or prostitutes, pot smokers, ex-cons, unwed mothers, or whatever) and (2) can identify her/himself as one of these kinds of labelable people, then it seems likely that the individual will self-label. It also seems likely that the self-

labeled individual will undergo many of the internal experiences of
the individual who is publicly labeled. Such an individual may also
learn to fear and/or expect the external, public experiences which
are overtly or covertly threatened for people of the kind (s)he can
be shown to be. Who has not seen, heard, or read about the reaction
of people to deviants: the obvious drunk, the "swish" man, or the
very "masculine" woman. It takes little imagination to realize that
negative societal reactions toward others can easily be directed
toward oneself if one is identified as deviant. As a result, the individual whose particular form of deviance is not obvious and yet is
generally defined, labeled, and reacted to by society might be expected to spend much time avoiding social labeling while at the same
time subscribing to and in fact organizing his/her life around a
definition of self as deviant.

Visibility

The degree to which a particular form of deviance is openly
exhibited and/or obvious, that is, its visibility, is another important
dimension of deviance. Goffman (1963) makes a distinction between
the "discredited" individual whose stigma is visible (such as the
person on crutches, or with a hearing aid, or white cane) and the
"discreditable" individual whose "virtual social identity" and "actual
social identity" are at odds, for example, the secret drinker or drug
user. Becker (1963) makes a similar distinction between what he
calls the "pure deviant" and the "secret deviant." The pure deviant
is one who engages in rule-breaking behavior and is perceived as
being deviant. The secret deviant engages in rule breaking but is
not perceived as being deviant. Visibility is not, however, an either/
or type of thing. An individual can be visible and thus a pure deviant
because there is something obvious about her/him to which society
reacts with a label, for example, some form of obvious physical
difference, defect, or disability. If the difference is not quite so
obvious, the individual may hover on the boundary between pure and
secret, discredited and discreditable, with neither the deviant nor
the observer quite sure whether the individual is or ought to be
labeled.

Deviance can thus be broken down according to its visibility
(pure or secret; discredited or discreditable) and the centrality of
its location in an individual's life (whether the individual's deviance
is primary or secondary). Obviously, the method of handling deviance will vary depending on where within this matrix the individual
falls. The person with a visible stigma (the discredited person) has
to cope with prejudice and discrimination.

> (b)ut for the (discreditable person) . . . it is not that
> he must face prejudice against himself, but rather he
> must face unwitting acceptance of himself by individuals
> who are prejudiced against persons of the kind he can
> be revealed to be. . . . By intention or in effect the
> (discreditable person) conceals information about his
> real social identity, receiving and accepting treatment
> based on false suppositions concerning himself (Goffman
> 1963, p. 42).

The individual with an invisible stigma, especially if it is
central to the self-image, may divide the world into those from whom
the stigma must be hidden, those who know about it but do not share
it, and those who share the stigma. With those who know about or
share the stigma, the deviant individual is, to varying degrees, free
to behave as (s)he wishes. With those who do not know and from
whom negative reactions and/or sanctions are anticipated, the deviant
individual who wishes to remain secret must "pass." To pass, to
appear to be someone different from whom one really is, requires
a great deal of management.

MANAGEMENT AND PASSING

Management of Day-to-Day Life

The process of managing a deviant identity involves dealing
with the interface between self as deviant and others as individuals
who might react to that deviance in negative ways. Garfinkel's (1967)
work shows the extent to which management involves an understanding
of the common sense, everyday meanings of day-to-day life on the
part of the manager (even if that person cannot articulate these understandings in sociological terms). Specifically, it is in part a process
of engaging in interactions either in such a way as to convey an
impression of self as nondeviant, or of dealing with the perspectives
or expected perspectives of others if one has already been identified
as a deviant. Garfinkel (1967, p. 137) elucidates some of the com-
plexities of such management in his study of Agnes, a person born
with external male genitalia but with the sexual identity of a normal
female:

> The work of achieving and making secure her rights to
> live as a normal, natural female while having continu-
> ally to provide for the possibilities of detection and
> ruin carried on within socially structured conditions I

call Agnes' 'passing.' Her situations of activity . . .
were chronically ones of "structured strain." We may
think of them as socially structured situations of potential and actual crisis. . . . Each of a great variety of
structurally different instances required vigilance,
resourcefulness, stamina, sustained motivation, pre-
planning that was accompanied continually by improvisa-
tion and, continually, sharpness, wit, knowledge, and
very importantly her willingness to deal in 'good
reasons'—i.e. to either furnish or be ready to furnish
reasonable justifications (explanations) or to avoid
situations where explanations would be required.
(Italics omitted)

The management of day-to-day life for any individual, not just
for the deviant, means that there are vast numbers of things that
must be taken for granted, assumed, and trusted in. Interactions
between people are based on their being able to assume that, for the
most part, "what you see is what you get," and that they can take on
trust the meaning of what they see. Garfinkel (1967, p. 173) points
out that for a person to be able to act rationally in day-to-day life

depends upon the person being able to take for granted,
to take under trust, a vast array of features of the
social order. In the conduct of his everyday affairs in
order for the person to treat rationally that one-tenth
of the situation that, like an iceberg appears above the
water, he must be able to treat the nine-tenths that lies
below as an unquestioned and . . . as an unquestionable
background of matters that are demonstrably relevant
to his calculation, but which appear without ever being
noticed.

Goffman (1963, 1967, 1974) has also pointed out in various contexts
that the possession or display of certain social characteristics (ego's
"face") entitles ego to expect others to treat him/her in a manner
appropriate to that face and to assume that (s)he is in fact the sort
of person (s)he claims to be or gives the appearance of being. It is
the near inevitability of this kind of taking-for-granted, this assumption that things are as they appear to be, that makes passing possible
for the social deviant.
    The work of passing, then, requires that the individual be able to
1) fit accurately into the world of the taken-for-granted, and 2) manifest characteristics which will lead others to value and treat her/him

in a way appropriate to her/his public, if not private, behavior. In order to achieve this, the deviant individual who is passing may find that routine, day-to-day activities as conditions "for the effective, calculated, and deliberate management of practical circumstances (are) . . . specifically and chronically problematic" (Garfinkel 1967, p. 175). That is to say, it is the ordinary, everyday world which can give the deviant trouble. The deviant is attempting to give off the right kind of impression to demonstrate to others that (s)he fits into the world-as-usual, that things are normal, that things can be taken for granted. In order to avoid suspicion, discovery, and labeling, the sexual deviant must act in ways that people who are not sexually deviant act; the alcoholic must figure out what nonalcoholics do that (s)he must do in order to appear nonalcoholic, the coworkers who are having a clandestine affair must act as people do who are not having an affair, and so on. Garfinkel (1967, p. 175) states that "the work of impression management (can be thought of) . . . as attempts to come to terms with practical circumstances as a texture of relevances over the continuing occasions of interpersonal transactions." He further points out that the passer becomes adept at the methodology of passing by knowing how "the organized features of ordinary settings are used by members as procedures for making appearances of (in this case) sexuality-as-usual decidable as a matter of course" (Garfinkel 1967, p. 175).

It is this knowledge about what makes things appear and be taken as matters of course that can be used by deviants (or anyone who wishes to deceive) to facilitate deceptions within various social frameworks. Goffman (1974, p. 251) states that

> (w)hatever it is that generates sureness is precisely
> what will be employed by those who want to mislead
> us. For surely, although some evidence will be much
> more difficult than other evidence to fake, and therefore
> will be of special use as a test of what is really going
> on, the more it is relied upon for this reason, the
> more reason there is to make the effort to fake it.

Thus, the deviant much more than the nondeviant must be sensitive to common sense understandings and behaviors in the areas relative to deviance in order to give off and maintain an impression of self as nondeviant.

Awareness Contexts

Such management does not involve the actor alone. "Any human activity involves an individual not only intentionally initiating action, but also imaginatively reconstructing the anticipated responses of others to that action" (Plummer 1975, p. 17). Furthermore, impression management is not always undertaken and when undertaken is not always successful. Management is not only a question of appearing normal, but of knowing that one has succeeded and of deciding what to do if one feels one has not succeeded, is not succeeding, or cannot succeed. It is also a matter which involves knowing with whom, to what extent and with regard to what impression management is necessary, and how effective one's attempt is likely to be.

In order to pass successfully, the individual needs to know how (s)he is perceived, what his/her identity is to self and to others. Glaser and Strauss (1964, p. 670) refer to this type of perceptive situation as an "awareness context." They describe an awareness context as "the total combination of what each interactant in a situation knows about the identity of the other and his own identity in the eyes of the other." Plummer (1975, p. 177) describes awareness contexts somewhat differently as

> attempt(s) to define situations by the nature and degree
> of distribution of social information . . . (they) take
> into account not only the simple questions of actual
> identity and information, but also those of imputed
> identity and information.

Scheff (1973) in attempting to combine his concepts of consensus and dissensus with the concept of awareness context found the notion of identity as used by Glaser and Strauss to be ill-defined and therefore problematic. His solution, and it seems like a good one, is to define identity itself in terms of the specific situation in which the interaction is taking place, that is, relative to the awareness context. He sees situational identity as being based on the part one plays in a given transaction, this part being mutually recognized by both parties to the transaction. Relationships he further defines as a collective term for situational identities in which "parties to a transaction have mutually recognized parts to play in the transaction" (Scheff 1973, p. 197).

Glaser and Strauss (1964) identify and Scheff (1973) utilizes four types of awareness context:

Open Context: Each interactant is aware of his/ her own identity and the identity of the other.

Closed Context: One interactant does not know either the other's identity or the other's view of her/his identity.

Suspicious Context: One interactant suspects the true
identity of the other or the other's
view of his/her identity, or both.

Pretense Context: Both interactants are fully aware,
but pretend not to be.

Some examples may serve to clarify the use of these concepts. For
the purposes of this paper, the use of lesbianism as an example will
serve to illustrate the point.

Open Context: Both parties know that the individual is a lesbian; each knows that
the other knows. In this type of
transaction, identity revolves
around those behaviors involved
in being "someone who is a lesbian"
and "someone who is relating to
someone who is a lesbian."

Closed Context: The lesbian knows who she is but
the other does not; or the other
knows that ego is a lesbian, but
ego doesn't know that alter knows.

Suspicious Context: Ego suspects that alter knows she
is a lesbian, or alter suspects that
ego is a lesbian, or both.

Pretense Context: Both parties know that ego is a
lesbian, but neither party admits
to the knowledge.

A relatively brief examination of these contexts in the light of
Garfinkel's conceptions and in terms of Scheff's definition of identity
and relationship will demonstrate that carrying out such relationships vis-a-vis the straight world could be complicated and involve
a good bit of management. Laing, Phillipson and Lee (1966) refer
to the types of perspectives and identities which may be involved in
such contextual interactions as "metaperspectives." That is, in any
interaction, I have my own view of myself; I have a perception or
view of the other; and I have my view of the other's view of me.
This last is what Laing et al. mean by a metaperspective; this is
ego's perception of the way (s)he is viewed by others and may affect
her/his behavior in that (s)he acts in ways which are influenced by

suppositions (which may or may not be accurate) concerning alter's attitudes, feelings, perceptions, and demands.

Along with the concept of metaperspective, they also introduce the concept of "metaidentity." Self-identity, they feel, involves not only ego's view of self, but also incorporates into that view the view of self ego thinks others have of her/him. Whether such a view is accepted or rejected, it still plays a part in self-identity if only insofar as to make the individual someone whose identity is that (s)he is a person who is thought of by alter in an incorrect way, that is, someone who is perhaps misunderstood by alter. Metaidentity involves my perception of myself based on the incorporation into my self-perception of my view of your view of me. If this sounds a bit like the queen in <u>Alice in Wonderland</u>, it might help to apply these concepts to the examples given above.

Open Context
Identity:	I am a lesbian. Alter is a straight person.
Metaidentity:	Alter sees me as a lesbian.
Perspective:	I am acting normal, but feel uptight about being a lesbian. Alter is acting cold.
Metaperspective:	Alter thinks that there's something wrong with me because I'm a lesbian. (S)he defines me as a sick person, as someone not to be trusted.

Closed Context
Identity:	I am a lesbian. Alter is a straight male.
Metaidentity:	Alter sees me as a straight person.
Perspective:	I'm acting normal. Alter is flirting.
Metaperspective:	Alter thinks it's strange that I don't pick up on his flirting. He's going to wonder what's wrong with me.

Suspicious Context
Identity:	I am a lesbian. Alter is a straight woman.
Metaidentity:	I think alter is wise to my being gay, but I'm not sure.

Perspective:	I am being cautious about revealing information about myself, because I'm not sure I trust her. Alter is curious.
Metaperspective:	Alter suspects that I'm a lesbian and is trying to find out by asking me questions about myself.

Pretense Context

Identity:	I am a lesbian. Alter is a straight person.
Metaidentity:	Alter knows I'm gay, and I know (s)he knows. (S)he probably interprets everything I do in terms of that, but neither of us lets on. I've been found out, but I can still act as though I haven't and alter doesn't want to confront the issue either, so we'll both play it safe.
Perspective:	I am acting as though I were straight, even though I know alter knows better. Alter is acting as though (s)he believes I'm straight even though she knows better.
Metaperspective:	Alter probably thinks everything I'm doing is fake, just because (s)he knows I'm gay.

It should be noted that, with reference to Scheff's notion of identity, the situational context in which interactions such as these take place is very important in determining both perspective and identity. One's perspective and identity in a work situation may be very different from one's perspective and identity at a party or with family. Related to awareness contexts, identities and perspectives and the day-to-day negotiation of reality are the concepts discussed earlier: 1) the individual's awareness of social labels; 2) the extent to which a particular type of deviance is a part of the individual's ongoing definition of self (we might consider this as the number of situations in which the deviance becomes part of the individual's identity and thus a part of the awareness context); and 3) the visibility of the particular form of deviance.

Garfinkel (1967) points out that passing is a day-to-day, ongoing process, and he contrasts his view with Goffman's situational analysis in which management tends to have a high degree of specificity. It is felt that both of these perspectives have validity and that both operate in the life of the individual. While the management of any given situation will depend on the specific situational context, the deviant is not merely a situational individual, but rather a person whose life has some flow and overlap from situation to situation. Particularly for the deviant who finds social support for his/her chosen life style, day-to-day activities are a mixture of easy and difficult situations, some requiring tricky maneuvers, some being second nature, and some requiring no management at all. Every individual at one time or another gets into a situation which requires special handling. Every individual manages his or her identity from day to day as roles and situational requirements change. What seems necessary is to somehow isolate specific situations and/or behaviors sufficiently to be able to analyze them without losing or minimizing the complexity, flow, and negotiability of ongoing social reality.

Appearing Normal

What must also be stressed is that the social deviant, like everyone else, operates in a world of "taken-for-granted . . . features of the social order." To do otherwise would breed chaos. The difference between the deviant and the nondeviant is one of degree, not necessarily of quality. As Becker (1963) and Erikson (1968) have pointed out, the social deviant engages in far more normal than abnormal behaviors, and these behaviors occur within the same contextual framework of ordinariness as the day-to-day behaviors of others. What become problematic are not the myriad unquestioned tasks and behaviors of ordinary living, but only those which can be related, sometimes quite obliquely, to the deviance in question. Impression management includes not only the control of impressions having to do with deviance, but, as Garfinkel has pointed out, of impressions having to do with the creation of the appearance of being normal. This is true whether the deviance is known or not. Even for the individual who cannot hide or perhaps willingly reveals his or her deviance, there may still be the necessity of coming to terms with social expectations. Sometimes this means living up to the expectations of others about how a deviant ought to behave (Erikson 1968; Goffman 1963); sometimes it means attempting to put the deviance in soft focus or making it nonthreatening (Goffman 1963). Any of these attempts can be viewed as social creations involving awareness contexts, identity, perspective, and a knowledge (or interpretation) of how to enact one's situational identity within a given context.

In reality, both passing and being deviant rely on the same processes. Numerous authors have pointed out the extent to which both labeling and the treatment of deviants are based on stereotyping and the generalization of expectations and definitions connected with a specific label (Becker 1963; Dinitz, Dynes, and Clarke 1969; Erikson 1962; Goffman 1963; Schur 1971; Scott 1972; Simmons 1969). It is this same process of generalization of expectation which operates in passing. If an individual can provide the right bits of information within a given situation to create a stereotype of normality, then (s)he can pass. The type of situation and the relationship of the interactants obviously affect how much and what kinds of work need to be done to create the appropriate stereotype. What must be realized is that the deviant does not utilize some magical skills or powers in order to appear normal, but rather uses an awareness of what is considered normal, of what will create the right impression, and this type of awareness is something shared to varying degrees by all interactants in the situation.

Much of passing seems to rely on the particular context of the interaction. For example, in a work or business context, an interaction between a man and a woman need not imply or include expectations about sexual relationships. Thus, the sexual preference of either may be said to be irrelevant to the context. All that either party needs to know how to do is behave appropriately vis-a-vis the work situation. However, if the man expects deference from women, and if the woman does not share his interpretation and is lesbian, she may feel that assertiveness or lack of deference on her part would be a clue that something is wrong. She may thus need to be sensitive to the man's expectations within the particular context and either exhibit a behavior she is not comfortable with, provide other information which will nullify the implications of her behavior, or be ready to deal with potentially unpleasant consequences. Notice here that both parties may be operating entirely on unsubstantiated assumptions about each other. The woman makes assumptions about the man's awareness, his perceptions of her, his expectations, his interpretations, and so forth. She may feel that, in the face of her assertiveness or nonresponsiveness, he suddenly becomes suspicious, thinks of her as too masculine, and then thinks of her as a lesbian (metaperspective). He, on the other hand, may simply be thinking of her as the type of woman he finds hard to deal with and may wonder how she gets along with her boyfriend, operating on the common male assumption that every woman has or wants a man.

It appears, then, that every situation can be seen before it is entered as requiring some given amount of management work. Some situations require none, some a great deal. Once in a situation, the changing context between interactants may require continual redefinition and negotiation of what is required to appear normal, or of whether to continue to maintain this appearance at all. Goffman (1963, p. 55) suggests that in such situations "characteristic discrepancies are likely to occur between virtual and actual social identity and characteristic efforts are made to manage the situation." We can now set out to look at the general ways in which such efforts can be made.

Management Work

On a gross level, each social situation or structure offers two possibilities for action: 1) the individual can avoid the situation whenever and wherever possible, or 2) the individual can enter the situation and attempt some kind of management. If the individual enters the situation, then management can involve either: 1) revealing one's deviance and coping with the response, or 2) attempting to pass. Passing is generally considered to mean that one hides that part of one's identity related to deviance. But passing may not be all that is involved in management. If we consider the concept of awareness contexts and the possible number of differing states of awareness, it seems that management may also involve not only assumptions about the awareness and expectations of the other, but the participation of the other as well. For example, in the situation where both interactants know that ego is a lesbian, but both act as if she were not, each relies on the other to continue the charade. Thus, management may involve not only attempting to hide one's deviance, but also attempting to enact and help others to enact pluralistic ignorance. The difficulty in this type of situation would seem to be that unless the issue has been broached, the deviant individual never knows for sure how alter will behave if the deviance becomes manifest and may never know whether alter is acting or ignorant.

In the instance in which the individual is actually trying to hide (that is, in which (s)he feels that (s)he is the only one who knows about the deviance), (s)he may need to do one or more of three things: 1) present valid information which will lead to an impression of nondeviance because of its supposed incompatibility with the deviance in question; 2) conceal or hide information and/or behavior which might lead others to question his/her identity; or 3) present false information or engage in faked behavior to support the impression of self as normal. To use lesbianism as an example, the first instance might involve referring to someone to whom one has actually been engaged, or to make passing references to an ex-lover (male), husband, or children, to express liking for or attraction to males, and so forth. In the second instance, the woman in question might simply not divulge the fact that she is living with another woman, or she might, when in public with her lover, refrain from open displays of affection. The third type of management might involve inventing a date with a man, referring to a lover or partner as "he" instead of "she," or telling about experiences with women as though they were men, and the like. A woman might also choose to dress and/or act in certain ways, for example, wearing very feminine clothing, flirting with men, and in general acting in ways which would contrast sharply with the public stereotype of lesbians and which would confirm the public stereotype of normal females. Whether these types of behavior would belong to category one or category three would depend upon how the individual felt about what she was doing. If she felt very natural dressing and behaving in a traditionally or stereotypically feminine way, then it would be an instance of using valid information to support an impression of normality. If the woman felt herself to be playacting, to be hiding her "real" self, or to be doing things under duress, then it might be considered false information.

SUMMARY

Thus far, this study has addressed deviance and deviance management in general. We have considered primary and secondary deviance, visibility, and passing in a general context. The preceding discussion has dealt with management and passing as complex interactions between the deviant individual and those others who might react to the deviance in negative ways. The author has tried to show the extent to which management may require an awareness of the everyday world of ordinary normal behavior, and an ability to engage in such behavior. An attempt has been made to show that management and passing depend on ego's awareness of the way (s)he is perceived in terms of her/his identity and of how a certain identity may get created. Identity has been viewed as a matter of situation definition, and we have looked at how identity and relationship interact in the case of deviance. Finally, we have talked briefly about the actual process of deviance management and some of the possible actions an individual might take in order to pass. We shall now turn to an exploration of the ways in which the concepts discussed in a general context can be applied specifically to lesbian women.

2

LESBIANISM

LESBIANISM AND PRIMARY DEVIANCE

Historically, lesbianism has been defined as sexual behavior. Webster (1972) defines lesbian as "a homosexual woman," and defines homosexual as being ". . . characterized by sexual desire for those of the same sex as oneself." Taber (1965, p. L–19) describes lesbianism as a "perversion in which sexual desire of women is only for one of their own sex." Given this type of definition, it seems obvious that the original (primary) deviant behavior involved in lesbianism would be a sexual act or the desire for a sexual act. Based on this act or the desire for it, and depending on her and/or others' reactions to it, a woman may or may not identify herself as lesbian and become involved in that life style. While lesbianism certainly does involve sexual behavior in many instances, it should be realized that definitions of lesbianism have frequently overlooked the emotional content of relationships between women and the extent to which this, even more than sexual behavior, can affect a woman's definition of herself (Abbott and Love 1972; Gagnon and Simon 1973b; Galana and Covina 1977).

Adolescence

Sexual behavior between women without necessary lesbian implications seems to occur most frequently during adolescence, and it is then that it is probably easiest to normalize for both the adolescent and others. Gagnon and Simon (1973a) report that in their study of college students, 6 percent of their sample had had homosexual contacts to orgasm and two-thirds of these (that is, 4

17

percent of the total sample) had the experience limited to adolescence. While the author does not know of any studies extant which discuss the ways in which straight women with adolescent homosexual experience manage to deal with this, the experiences of lesbian women suggest that if the encounters become known they are frequently dismissed as "going through a stage" or they may be ignored or actively forgotten (see Abbott and Love 1972, and Galana and Covina 1977, for example).

"Going through a stage" is probably the interpretation most frequently given to the teenage crush, often the first emotional experience of lesbianism for women who later become committed to a lesbian life style (Gagnon and Simon 1973a). Such relationships are frequently seen as a normal part of female adolescence. Douvan (1970), for example, stresses the importance of like-sexed friendships for girls during adolescence and points out that in these relationships girls develop a greater intimacy and maturity than do boys in their like-sexed relations. Abbott and Love (1972, p. 24) state that

> adolescent girls commonly experience crushes on
> teachers, older girls or female classmates. . . .
> These bonds are seen as normal until the age for dating
> boys arrives—and now that age can sometimes be as
> early as eleven or twelve. A girl is expected to grow
> out of all this and learn to transfer her love and trust
> to men.

If such emotional attachments are terminated at the right time and if the young woman develops appropriate interests in dating, marriage, and other feminine things, adolescent involvements may be successfully normalized and need not lead to labeling. In fact such involvements may play an important part in preparing the adolescent girl for her future role as a straight woman (Douvan 1970).

Another way of normalizing such behavior in the late adolescent or early adult years is to view it in the context of other sex-related or sexual behavior which is "normal." The author has talked with a number of lesbian women who reported that, before coming out, close relationships were handled acceptably by double-dating or by simply considering these women as close friends. The relationship and the emotions were legitimized because either one or both girls were concurrently dating boys. As long as heterosexual involvements continue, the woman who forms strong attractions for and attachments to other women can reassure herself and convince others that she is not deviant. Some women carry this to the point of getting married and having children while either continuing their relationships with women or putting these relationships aside temporarily (see, for example, Galana and Covina 1977; Johnston 1973).

Not all adolescents are willing or able to adapt to societal pressures to act "normal," or they may act in socially acceptable ways while wishing to behave differently and feeling inwardly that something is wrong. In either case, the adolescent lesbian may find herself in a particularly isolated situation and is liable to be labeled early by self, others, or both as "queer." When this happens, the family which should be a source of protection and support may become instead a source of fear and alienation (see Simpson 1976, pp. 14–32, for example).

Situational Requirements

Another way to normalize sexual or emotional involvement with a woman is to consider it as part of the situational requirements. Giallombardo (1966), for example, reported on women in prisons where she found that, although many women adopted lesbian-type (that is, emotional and sexual) relationships with other women in the prison setting, these were simply to make the prison term "easy time." They were not considered to be permanent or to take the place of heterosexual attachments outside of prison. In fact, Giallombardo reports that women who came into prison as lesbians were ostracized because theirs was a permanent choice rather than one of necessity.

It seems, then, that if strong emotional and/or sexual attachments between women coincide with or give way at the appropriate time to attachments with men, they can be viewed as normal, or at least normalizable, and need not imply permanent deviance on the part of the women involved. However, if the individual finds that her interest in women continues, that it conflicts with her interest in men, and/or that she is not interested in the traditional feminine role, she may be on her way toward conceiving of herself as lesbian and of becoming a secondary deviant.

LESBIANISM AND SECONDARY DEVIANCE

Gagnon and Simon (1973a) found that women who became lesbian frequently identified themselves as different during adolescence or even in early childhood and that such women often labeled that feeling of difference as homosexuality by hearing conversations or reading books about homosexuality and lesbianism. Abbott and Love (1972, p. 25) put it somewhat more dramatically:

At some point, of course, she will begin to wonder if she is different from most of the women around her

and what her difference means. She may go to the
library, to a counselor, psychiatrist, or minister to
find out about her feelings. What she reads on the
pages of a psychology book, what she sees on the face
of a family doctor or minister, may reverberate through
the rest of her life. The jokes and references heard on
the playground, in the street, or at home grow clearer.
She still may not know the proper name for what she is,
but she knows the slang for it; she knows she is 'queer.'

It seems that in most instances which are reported women who
come to identify themselves as lesbian do so first by identifying something different about themselves and then by putting a name to this
difference. In some cases, the name is actively assigned from outside, but this does not seem to be generally the case. Nor is the
awareness of difference most often a sudden one.

It doesn't just happen to you. It isn't as if you wake up
suddenly one morning and say to yourself, 'I am a
lesbian.' Or that you make a conscious decision—'that
is what I'm going to be from now on'—as if it were an
acceptable goal in life. . . . It's rather like a slowly
emerging awareness of [oneself] as someone who is
different, who is responding in ways that are apparently
not usual to others and yet seem very natural to [one-
self] (Martin and Lyon 1972, p. 22).

Frequently, the discovery of sexual desire for another woman can
create extreme conflict between the rightness and joy of the experience itself and its apparent wrongness when placed in a societal
context.

. . . I was still in love with my first woman and somehow I began to develop the idea that something was
wrong with me and I'd better take charge of myself and
do something about it. Obviously something was
wrong. . . . It wasn't all right, but it was. It wasn't
all right because it was completely hushed up, I never
could mention it to my collegemates, even my close
friend or two, even my roommate; and my lover herself,
being one of my teachers, was in mortal fear of dis-
closure. So naturally it was not all right. It couldn't
possibly have been all right when all the others were
boasting about their boyfriends and even flaunting their
relationships in public or making big fusses about a

date or a blind date or a letter or a phone call. I made
my affair all right to myself in private by the sheer
undeniable extent of my passion. This woman was a
greatly respected teacher, too. So of course it was
all right. I was actually very proud to be involved with
such a woman. Thus, I was able to overlook being
wrong (Johnston 1973, p. 50).

The awareness of who one is, of what it means to be a lesbian,
may involve a struggle with the socially tailored definition of lesbians
put together by both straight and gay societies. Johnston (1973, p. 58)
describes a part of the difficulty in defining a lesbian identity:

> . . . there was lesbian activity, no lesbian identity.
> Everybody understood identity. When you filled out
> application blanks for schools or jobs, you found out
> who you were or who you could be. You were male or
> female, single, married or divorced, protestant or
> catholic, old or young, white or black, and anglo or
> jewish. And you had a name. Identity is what you can
> say you are according to what they say you can be.
> And not the least of the categories of identity is that
> of sexual status under the law which allowed of no
> other orientation than that of heterosexuality. Lesbian
> identity was a criminal or non-identity (Italics added).

To define oneself as a lesbian, unless one is fortunate enough to live
in an area where lesbianism is relatively visible and relatively
acceptable, has until recently meant resorting to the psychological
literature or to one of a number of rather maudlin books like Well
of Loneliness (Hall 1950) or We Walk Alone (Aldrich 1955), and
supplementing this meagre fare with the definition conveyed through
magazines and newspapers, conversation, jokes, movies, porno-
graphic literature, and the like.
    Although the definition of lesbianism is primarily sexual, the
social conception of lesbianism is much broader (as is the reality
of being a lesbian) and includes notions about appearance, behavior,
personality, and so forth. Many of these assumptions, for example,
the idea that lesbians assume strict "butch" and "femme" roles have
been perpetuated by the lesbian community itself as well as by others
(Abbott and Love 1972; Klaich 1974; Martin and Lyon 1972; Wysor
1974). As has been mentioned earlier, many of those writing on
lesbians and homosexuals have also assumed an inherent pathology
or dysfunction (for example, Bergler 1957; Bieber 1962; Bieber 1976;
Caprio 1954; Gnepp 1975).

While these assumptions and stereotypes are changing, change comes slowly both within and outside of the lesbian community. Klaich (1974), for example, summarizes the results of a number of surveys done in the United States in the late 1960s and early 1970s which show that, on the whole, the attitudes of people in this country toward homosexuals are still strongly negative. Other indications of the difficulty of changing the conception of lesbianism (and homosexuality) can be seen in the recent American Psychological Association (APA) controversy over removing homosexuality from the diagnostic manual (DSM-II) where it had been classified as a sexual deviation and in the numerous court battles which have occurred across the country (Gnepp 1975; Hadden 1976; Meyer 1977).

When the lesbian woman "comes out," that is, when she identifies herself to herself and to others as a lesbian, she may find that she has begun a process which increasingly affects her life. She has identified herself as a person toward whom society as a whole still holds predominantly negative attitudes. Her friendships and social life may begin to include primarily gay people, she may become acquainted with gay bars, and may if she chooses enter an afterhours world which largely excludes men and straight people. She has also entered a situation in which her sexual preference and her life style may frequently be matters for concern when she is at work or in the company of straight people. Her lesbianism cannot be taken for granted in the way that heterosexuality is by straights. Although others may be willing and even very much inclined to take her as heterosexual, the business of creating an appearance which will enable others to do this is, as has been shown earlier, potentially problematic. The extent to which this is problematic should be closely related to how visible the lesbian woman is or feels she is.

LESBIANISM AND VISIBILITY

Plummer (1975, p. 179) states that

(r)ecognition of homosexuality depends upon both perception and action: somebody must identify a homosexual, and certain actions must be identifiable as homosexual. With the exception of being caught in the act, there is nothing automatic and intrinsic about such recognition processes; they depend largely upon the mediation of certain patterns of socially constructed meanings.

Following Kitsuse (1962), Plummer notes that there are two ways for homosexuals to be identified: direct visibility and indirect visibility. Direct visibility includes discovery, denunciation, and declaration, while indirect visibility includes stereotypical symmetry and rumor.

Discovery

The lesbian is probably even less likely than the male homosexual to be "discovered" in a sexual act. However, there is always a possibility that she may be discovered in a local bar or other known watering place by someone straight and be directly visible in this way.

Denunciation

This is also another unlikely way of becoming directly visible for lesbian women, although it certainly occurs. Perhaps the most frequent instances of denunciation occur relative to lesbian mothers who are denounced by husbands or neighbors in order to protect the children (see, for example, Martin and Lyon 1972, pp. 140-76 and Galana and Covina 1977, pp. 15-21).

Declaration

This is a way of being directly visible that seems to be chosen by increasing numbers of individuals, particularly with the advent and growth of the Gay Liberation Movement (Jay and Young 1975). Lesbian women may choose to be quite forthright with everyone about their preferences or to tell only selected people. There is always the possibility, of course, that there will be social repercussions to declaring oneself a lesbian, and there are certainly problems encountered in social interactions when one is known to be gay. Nonetheless, this is apparently an increasingly utilized solution to the problem of managing an identity as a secret deviant.

Stereotypical Symmetry

No matter how small the percentage of women who fit the stereotype of a lesbian, there are inevitably women who do or who are afraid that they do. Lesbianism is something which encompasses not only sexual, but sex-role behavior, and so the lesbian woman who is single, has short hair, affects "masculine" clothing, walks in a style not particularly feminine, and is assertive into the bargain, may be concerned that she is visible whether she is or not.

Rumor

Another common way for an individual to become visible is through rumor as was found by both Kitsuse (1962) and Schofield (1973). Although in itself a way of becoming visible, rumor would seem to be based on other types of visibility, for example, stereotypy, or the observation of the individual at a bar or with a group of women who are judged to be gay, or to the absence of expected behaviors such as dating, flirting, or mate seeking.

In any event, the lesbian woman is much more likely to be discreditable or secret than discredited because for the most part, lesbians look and act like other women, especially when under public scrutiny (Abbott and Love 1972; Goode and Troiden 1974; Martin and Lyon 1972; Wysor 1974). The fact that being a lesbian frequently involves an entire life style, however, means that visibility and thus the possibility of rumor is not only a question of appearance or of being seen in the wrong place or with the wrong people. The pervasive assumption of heterosexuality frequently carries with it other assumptions about how one spends or wishes to spend one's time, about one's behavior, life style, goals, needs, and the like. For the lesbian woman, the management of everyday life may include a large portion of behavior that most straight people take for granted. For example, it is generally assumed that a single woman is looking for a husband and that she has or is looking for a boyfriend, that she dates men, and so forth. A single woman who is not engaged in any of these pursuits may feel that she is somewhat conspicuous and may worry that people will put together various bits of information about her: her single status, female roommate, lack of dating behavior, and so forth, and come to the conclusion that she is a lesbian. Because of this, the lesbian woman who is trying to remain unidentified may need to actively engage in identity management and passing.

LESBIANISM, MANAGEMENT, AND PASSING

When all of the factors discussed so far in this chapter are put together, the process of deviance management for a lesbian woman can be seen to be potentially very complicated. Because the purpose of this study is really to fill in this section, that is, to begin to elucidate the process of management, the major consideration of these issues will be reserved for the discussion section so that it will be possible to include data gathered in the present study. What must now be done is to raise some of the specific issues and assumptions relative to lesbian women which are germane to the research at hand.

The basic conception thus far proposed is that deviance in general and lesbianism in particular are problematic in large part because of societal reactions to labels. The process of labeling, however, is not conceived of necessarily as a one-shot affair, although it may be so. Particularly for the individual whose deviance is not readily visible, labeling is a matter of management and negotiation between the deviant and others (both deviant and nondeviant) with whom (s)he comes in contact and within the deviant her or himself. Management (and frequently labeling) can thus really be conceived of as a process; as a series of choices, decisions, actions, and interactions. The individual must decide how to act in various circumstances in order to present a desired image to those, including the individual him/herself, who can label. For the lesbian woman, one general category of options for management is the decision to pass, that is, to avoid the label "lesbian." At present, there are no data to indicate what women do or avoid doing in order to pass, what situations they find difficult, or whether there are any variables which would seem to make management and/or passing easy or difficult.

It was felt in beginning this study that two factors which might affect the ease of management would be self-perceived visibility (how readily a woman thinks she can be identified as a lesbian) and heterosexual experience. Visibility was felt to be relevant in that it was expected that a woman who did not feel highly visible or identifiable as a lesbian would need to be less concerned about being identified and therefore have less difficulty in managing her lesbianism. Heterosexual experience and marital status were considered important for similar reasons. First, it seemed likely that the more heterosexual experience a woman had the more skills she would have which would be applicable in situations calling for straight (that is, nonlesbian) behavior. Thus, the management of day-to-day situations in which such behavior was generally expected ought to be easier for these women. Second, the woman with more heterosexual experience had information at her disposal which could be used to produce assumptions about her normality, particularly if she had been married. It seemed likely that women who could, if they wished, refer to husbands, boyfriends, lovers, children, and the like, would find it easier to create an expectation or assumption of heterosexuality than women who did not have such experiences to draw on.

Although management is assumed to vary somewhat from situation to situation, it is also assumed (for want of any clear indicators otherwise) that management ease or difficulty should be something which cuts across situations. Management for this study was defined as the process of engaging in specific behaviors in order to be taken as heterosexual and/or avoiding situations and behaviors which would be likely to identify a woman as lesbian. For the purposes of this study, management was divided into four categories:

1. The degree to which a woman rates different situations as difficult because of being lesbian (greater difficulty = greater management).

2. The number of such situations which she actively avoids (more situations avoided = greater management).

3. The degree to which a woman engages in behaviors which would cause her to be seen as straight (greater number of behaviors = greater management) and avoids behaviors which might cause her to be identified as lesbian (more behaviors avoided = greater management).

4. The degree to which a woman feels free to engage in various risk-taking behaviors (that is, behaviors which might cause her to be identified as lesbian) in various situations (fewer behaviors = greater management).

HYPOTHESES AND DESCRIPTIVE DATA

The following hypotheses were tested in the current study.

Hypothesis I

The more a woman feels that she can be identified as a lesbian and the more concerned she is about being so identified, the more management she will engage in. Specifically, the more a woman feels identifiable and the more concerned she is:

Hypothesis IA: The more difficulty she will report in various social situations involving straight people.

Hypothesis IB: The more social situations involving straight people she will avoid.

Hypothesis IC: The greater the number of behaviors she will engage in (or avoid) around straight people to keep from being identified as lesbian.

Hypothesis ID: The fewer risk-taking behaviors she will feel free to engage in around straight people which might cause her to be identified as lesbian.

Hypothesis II

The more heterosexual experience a woman has, the less management she will engage in. Specifically, the more heterosexual experience a woman has:

Hypothesis IIA: The less difficulty she will report in various social situations involving straight people.

Hypothesis IIB: The fewer the number of social situations involving straight people she will avoid.

Hypothesis IIC: The fewer behaviors she will engage in (or avoid) around straight people in order to keep from being identified as lesbian.

Hypothesis IID: The greater the number of risk-taking behaviors she will feel free to engage in around straight people which might cause her to be identified as lesbian.

Descriptive Data

As well as testing the above hypotheses, the study was also designed to gather purely descriptive data on, among other things, number and types of relationships with both gay and straight people, types of management efforts undertaken by the women in the sample, respondents' perceptions of their own visibility, attitudes toward being lesbian, and positive and negative aspects to being a lesbian woman. These data were felt to be equally as important as the tests of the hypotheses in describing the management efforts of women in the sample and are therefore presented in detail in the data section.

3

METHODOLOGY

In studying members of a population whose defining characteristic makes them both vulnerable and frequently unlikely to identify
themselves as members of that population, any kind of representative
sample is virtually impossible. The majority of studies of homosexuals and lesbians have relied either on close contact with the community (for example, Cory 1965; Warren 1972) or have utilized special
populations, for example, women in prison (Ward and Kassebaum
1964; Giallombardo 1966), and women in therapy (Caprio 1954; Deutsch
1933; Gundlach and Riess 1968). None of the samples in the studies
done to date can be considered to be representative of the lesbian
population in the United States. Obviously, then, any sample taken
from a population which remains anonymous by choice (if not by
necessity) and which is based either on volunteerism or captivity
must be highly limited in its generalizability. In considering a study
such as this one, it is necessary to balance the inevitability of a
biased sample against the absence of any data at all.

SUBJECTS

The sample obtained for this study is what Babbie (1975) calls
a "snowball sample." Individuals known to the author were used as
sources for other possible interviewees and, by asking women who
took the questionnaire to suggest other women who might take it or
be willing to distribute it, the sample snowballed. While this type
of sample is obviously biased in that it relies for its start on women
known to the author, it is believed that the sample ultimately included
individuals with diverse backgrounds and experiences.

29

Three hundred questionnaires were distributed in California, Ohio, and New York during the late spring and early summer of 1975. Of these 300, 82 were returned. One questionnaire had to be thrown out because it was not sufficiently completed.

The subjects were all women. They ranged in age from 20 to 54 with a mean age of 32 years. Level of education ranged from high school or less to post doctorate. Ninety·percent of the women studied were currently employed in occupations as diverse as college professor, gardener, housemaid, hairdresser, school teacher, auto mechanic, and self-employed businesswoman. The great majority (80 percent) of the women in the sample were currently involved with a lover or partner and 67 percent of these (53 percent of the sample) were living together. About 68 percent of these women had been involved with their current partner for at least a year (N = 36), and almost 23 percent of the sample had been involved with their present partner for five years or more (N = 14). Twenty percent of the sample (N = 16) had never lived with another woman and almost 9 percent of the sample (N = 7) had never been involved with another woman at all, although they defined themselves as lesbian.

There are three major factors which must be considered when viewing the results of this study and considering their generalizability. First, all of these women have close enough connections with other lesbian women to have been reached by the sampling method used. This means that in all probability, because of the way the sample was obtained, respondents are: 1) involved to some extent with the lesbian community; they are not isolates, and may thus differ from other lesbian women who are less involved with the lesbian community; 2) even though they are involved, they do not appear to be radical and thus probably do not represent adequately that growing portion of the lesbian community which is radical; and 3) they are probably more similar to the researcher than they would have been in a probability sample.

Second, the great majority of these women (88 percent) live in California, a state which has relatively large enclaves of lesbian women in both northern and southern regions and which, with cities like Los Angeles and San Francisco, is almost without a doubt more supportive of alternative life styles (and probably has more of them) than other states. This may mean that the management problems of these women, their attitudes toward lesbianism and toward themselves as lesbian women, their experiences with other lesbian women and with straight people all may differ greatly from the experiences, attitudes and problems of women in more repressive areas of the country.

The third factor which must be considered is that this questionnaire was directed almost exclusively to lesbian women in partnerships. This was an oversight on the part of the researcher and one which also limits the generalizability of the results. This focus unfortunately discouraged some women who were not currently involved with another woman from completing the questionnaire. Those women not currently in relationships who did complete the questionnaire frequently mentioned that they had difficulty with this aspect. All seemed to have proceeded on an "as if" basis. Therefore, these data really apply for the most part to women who are in monogamous relationships rather than to those who prefer not to be or who are perhaps in a state of transition.

It should be mentioned that in obtaining this sample a conscious attempt was made to avoid those resources so frequently used in studying lesbian women: therapists, students, and lesbian women's associations like the Daughters of Bilitis. In so doing it was hoped that a different type of sample might be obtained than is usually tapped in studies of lesbian women.

It must be stressed that the results of this study have a limited generalizability. The sample is too small and the likelihood of bias too great to allow for assumptions of external validity. At best, therefore, we could hope that the sample is similar to a predominantly white population, essentially middle-class California lesbian women and that from it we could make some informed guesses about the population from which it was drawn.

PROCEDURE

A self-administered questionnaire was used for data collection (Appendix A). A cover letter noted that the researcher is, herself, a lesbian. It was hoped that this would encourage respondents to be more honest than they might be with a straight researcher and would also increase the number of women who would be willing to respond. The questionnaires were administered in a variety of ways. Some were passed out by the author and collected immediately; some were left in bars and women's centers in the Bay Area. By far the largest number were distributed by mail, including those in Ohio and the majority of those in southern California. Stamped, self-addressed envelopes were included with all questionnaires so they could be returned to the author anonymously without expense on the part of respondents.

MEASUREMENT

Independent Variables

Hypothesis I

The independent variables for Hypothesis I were self-perceived visibility and concern about being identified by straight people. Self-perceived visibility was measured by using two questions. The first question (Measure 1) was the score assigned to the respondent on the following question: "Do you think that straight people can tell that you're gay?" (Appendix A, Question 29). On the second question (Measure 2), respondents were asked to choose from a list of 14 items those things which they felt might cause straight people to identify them as lesbian (Appendix A, Question 32). An individual's score was the total number of items checked. Concern about being identified (Measure 3) was obtained from respondents' scores on the following question: "When you are around straight people, how often do you think about whether they will know you're gay?" (Appendix A, Question 30).

Hypothesis II

Two measures of heterosexual experience were used. The first was marital status (Appendix A, Question 6). Respondents were divided into two groups on the basis of whether or not they had ever been married. The second measure of heterosexual experience was the Kinsey scale (Kinsey 1953) (Appendix A, Question 15). For purposes of analysis, the Kinsey scale was made into a dichotomous variable. All individuals with scores of 5 and 6 were combined into a low experience group, while individuals with scores of 4 and below were combined to create a high experience group.

Dependent Variables

Hypotheses IA and IIA

The question used to determine the degree of difficulty women experienced in situations with straight people listed 15 situations which respondents were asked to rate in terms of difficulty (Appendix A, Question 35). Each situation was looked at separately on the basis of its difficulty. Two composite scores were also calculated for each respondent: Mean Difficulty and Number of Difficult Situations. The first composite score consisted of the sum of all ratings given by the respondent divided by the total number of situations rated (this total was not always 15 as not all situations applied to all applicants). The second composite score was obtained by totaling the number of situations each respondent rated as <u>at least</u> somewhat difficult, that is, with a score of 3 or less (1 = extremely difficult; 2 = quite difficult; 3 = somewhat difficult).

Hypotheses IB and IIB

The number of situations avoided was determined by tallying the number of situations circled by respondents (Appendix A, Question 36).

Hypotheses IC and IIC

In order to determine what kinds of behaviors lesbian women engaged in to hide the fact of being lesbian, respondents were given a list of behaviors and asked which of these they had ever engaged in to hide the fact of being lesbian (Appendix A, Question 39). The number of items checked was totaled to give a score for each individual.

Hypotheses ID and IID

In order to determine how much freedom respondents would feel to engage in certain "risk-taking" behaviors around straight individuals, a fairly complex question was used. Respondents were given seven situations and were asked to indicate for each situation which of seven different types of behavior they would feel free to engage in with a lover or partner (Appendix A, Question 38). Five of the situations listed involved straight people, two of the situations involved other gay people. The behaviors included: showing physical affection, showing verbal affection, using nicknames, terms of endearment, and the like, discussing the relationship, interacting on a "personal" level, using joint pronouns (for example, "we," "our"), and being in close physical proximity.

Each situation was looked at separately in terms of the numbers of behaviors respondents felt free to engage in, and a composite score was also developed for each behavior across four of the situations involving straight people. Only the first four situations were used (Appendix A, Question 38, A, B, C, and D) for each subject because there were no significant differences among these situations in terms of numbers of behaviors respondents felt free to engage in, but there were differences between these situations and situations E, F and G. These were the four situations in which the straight person did <u>not</u> know that the respondent was lesbian.

Other Measures

Others' Knowledge

Respondents were given a list of individuals and asked to indicate, first, which of these individuals they <u>thought</u> knew they were gay, and second, which of these individuals they were <u>sure</u> knew they were gay because they had either told them or discussed it with them (Appendix A, Question 16). These data were used to determine how many respondents had actually "come out" and to whom.

Social Relationships

Questions were asked to determine how much contact respondents had both with other lesbian women and with straight people. To determine the amount of contact with straight people, two questions were asked. First, respondents were asked to indicate how much contact they had with straight people at work (Appendix A, Question 18). Second, respondents were asked how often they saw straight people socially (Appendix A, Question 19).

Two questions were asked to get a measure of respondents' contacts with other lesbian women. First, they were asked how often they saw other gay women socially (Appendix A, Question 27). Second, they were asked how often they went to gay bars (Appendix A, Question 28).

Attitudes toward Being Lesbian

Three questions were asked to determine certain aspects of the way respondents viewed being lesbian. First, respondents were asked whether or not they liked being lesbian (Appendix A, Question 33). Second, respondents were asked to what extent they felt that being lesbian was a definite choice as opposed to being something they couldn't help (Appendix A, Question 34). Finally, respondents were given a list of nine possible advantages to having relationships with women rather than with men and asked to rate each one on a 5-point scale (Appendix A, Question 40).

Open-ended Questions

A number of open-ended questions were asked which, it was hoped, would fill any gaps left by the closed-ended questions. Four of these questions asked respondents to describe management issues (Appendix A, Questions 41, 43, 46, and 47). One question asked respondents specifically for positive aspects of being lesbian (Appendix A, Question 42). Two questions were used to determine what the experience of being lesbian was like in general—important, irrelevant, positive, and so on (Appendix A, Questions 44 and 45). Finally, two questions were asked which gave respondents a chance to relate ways in which they might have answered the questionnaire differently at a previous time (Appendix A, Question 48) and to add anything that they wished (Appendix A, Question 49).

These questions were not used as "hard" data; no analyses were run using these questions; they were not considered to be measures of variables. The primary purpose in asking them was to use them to add some flesh to the frequently bare bones of survey data. Although categories of responses were tallied for those questions where it seemed appropriate to do so, the responses were used largely verbatim in the discussion section of the study to illustrate points made by the data or to highlight various issues.

4

RESULTS

The measures of both independent and dependent variables in this study were developed and utilized not only to test the hypotheses, but to provide descriptive data as well. Consequently, the data obtained on the independent and dependent variables alone are presented first, followed by data relevant to the hypotheses, and finally, data are presented on the other measures described in the Measurement section of the preceding chapter. In presenting these data, the author wishes again to remind the reader that the smallness of the sample combined with a lack of representativeness severely limits the extent to which the findings can be generalized beyond the sample itself. In spite of these shortcomings, however, the results are thought-provoking and have been treated and discussed according to the author's belief that they are not highly idiosyncratic to the sample but are reflective of a broader reality. Unfortunately, there is no way to provide the reader with any assurance of a statistical nature that this is indeed the case.

INDEPENDENT VARIABLES

As described earlier, there were two sets of independent measures, those related to visibility and those related to heterosexual experience. The data relevant to visibility will be presented first.

Visibility

Measure 1

Measure 1 asked respondents to indicate how often they felt
that they could be identified as lesbian by straight people. The mean
response was 2.65 on a 5-point scale (5 = almost always; 1 = never),
indicating that respondents as a whole did not feel highly visible. In
fact, 41 percent of the sample fell into the lowest two categories
indicating that they thought they were seldom (N = 24) or never (N = 9)
visible (Table 4.1). In contrast, only 15 percent of the sample felt
that they were often (N = 10) or almost always (N = 2) visible.

Measure 2

The women in the sample did not report thinking about being
identified when around straight people to any great extent (Table 4.2).
The mean response was 2.76 on a 5-point scale (5 = almost always;
1 = never). Almost 44 percent of the sample said they seldom (N = 32)
or never (N = 3) thought about being identified as contrasted with only
19 percent of the sample who said they often (N = 11) or almost always
(N = 4) thought about being identified.

TABLE 4.1

Measure 1: Frequency with Which Respondents Felt
That Straights Could Identify Them as Lesbian

Response (Scale Value)		N	Percent*
Never	(1)	9	11
Seldom	(2)	24	30
Sometimes	(3)	34	42
Often	(4)	10	12
Almost always	(5)	2	3

Mean = 2.65
Variance = .873
S.D. = .934
*Rounded to nearest percent.
Source: Compiled by the author.

TABLE 4.2

Measure 2: Frequency with Which Respondents Thought
about Being Identified When around Straights

Response (Scale Value)		N	Percent*
Never	(1)	3	4
Seldom	(2)	32	40
Sometimes	(3)	30	38
Often	(4)	11	14
Almost always	(5)	4	5

Mean = 2.76
Variance = .842
S.D. = .917
*Rounded to nearest percent.
Source: Compiled by the author.

Measure 3

Respondents were asked to indicate what personal characteristics they felt could tip straights off that they were gay (Table 4.3).
Of the 13 items given, the item checked most frequently was "single
status." Forty-six percent of the respondents (N = 37) felt that this
could tip straights off. The next most frequently checked item was
"interests" (41 percent; N = 33). The items least often checked were
"too many masculine characteristics" and "body build." The mean
number of items checked was 3.87. Respondents were given the
opportunity to write in other responses but only two or three respondents did so.

Relationships among Independent Measures

Correlations were run among the three independent measures
in order to determine whether they were related (Table 4.4). Significant correlations were obtained, but they were low. Measure 1 and
Measure 2 had a correlation of .22 (p < .03) indicating that the more
likely a woman was to think she could be identified, the more she
thought about being identified around straights. Measure 1 and
Measure 3 had a correlation of .35 (p < .001) which suggested that

TABLE 4.3

Measure 3: Personal Characteristics Respondents Felt
Could Tip Straights Off That They Were Gay

Characteristic	N	Percent*
Single status	37	46
Interests	33	41
Reaction to women	24	30
Reaction to men	24	30
Way of walking	22	27
Hair style	22	27
Way of talking	22	27
Lack of feminine characteristics	22	27
Stance	17	21
Way of sitting	15	18
Occupation	13	16
Body build	9	11
Too many masculine characteristics	8	10

Mean number of items checked 3.87
Variance   3.11
S.D.   1.76
*Rounded to the nearest percent.
Source: Compiled by the author.

TABLE 4.4

Correlations among Independent Measures

Correlation	r	r^2	p
Measure 1 × Measure 2	.22	.04	.03
Measure 1 × Measure 3	.35	.12	.001
Measure 2 × Measure 3	.30	.09	.003

Source: Compiled by the author.

the more things a woman thought could tip others off, the more likely she was to feel identifiable. Finally, Measure 2 and Measure 3 had a correlation of .30 (p < .003) which showed that the more things a woman felt could tip straights off, the more likely she was to think about being identified when around straights. It should be noted, however, that none of the relationships explained more than 12 percent of the existing variance, indicating that while they were statistically significant they weren't very strong.

Heterosexual Experience

Measure 4

This measure was fairly straightforward and used the Kinsey scale as a measure of heterosexual experience (Table 4.5). Eighty-five percent of the sample (N = 69) had had both homosexual and heterosexual experiences, while 14 percent had had experiences exclusively with one sex or the other (N = 12). The majority of those with both types of experience had had largely homosexual and either distinct (N = 30; 37 percent) or incidental (N = 27; 33 percent) heterosexual experience.

TABLE 4.5

Sexual Experience as Measured by the Kinsey Scale

Sexual Experience		N	Percent
Entirely heterosexual	(0)	2	2
Largely heterosexual with incidental homosexual	(1)	2	2
Largely heterosexual with distinct homosexual	(2)	7	9
About equal	(3)	3	4
Largely homosexual with distinct heterosexual	(4)	30	37
Largely homosexual with incidental heterosexual	(5)	27	33
Entirely homosexual	(6)	10	12

Source: Compiled by the author.

Measure 5

This measure asked respondents for their marital status. For purposes of analysis, this was made into a dichotomous variable with only two categories: ever married and never married. Eighteen percent of the respondents (N = 5) had been or were currently married.

DEPENDENT VARIABLES

As described earlier, there were four dependent variables used in this study, all of which were intended to reflect ease or difficulty of management either in terms of behaviors or situational factors. Although the purpose of these measures was primarily for hypothesis testing, the data gathered are of interest per se and are presented below.

Situational Difficulty

On this variable, a low score indicated great difficulty and a high score indicated little difficulty using a 5-point scale. Of the 15 situations given, those which were considered most difficult were "having relatives to your home" ($\overline{X}$ = 3.45), "going to a straight party with your partner" ($\overline{X}$ = 3.45), and "going to a straight party alone" ($\overline{X}$ = 3.61) (Appendix B, Table B.1). Interestingly enough, none of the items received a mean rating lower than 3 (that is, more than somewhat difficult). The composite measure of number of items rated as at least somewhat difficult (that is, with a score of 3 or less) had a mean of 3.06, and the average mean overall for all situations combined was 4.14.

An open-ended question was also included to give respondents an opportunity to write in any situations which they found particularly difficult which were not mentioned in the list. Thirty women wrote in responses. Seven women said they had difficulty in situations involving straight men. For example, one woman said it was difficult "generally being around straight men or in a situation in which I could be considered available for straight men to pick up." Six women said they found it difficult to display physical affection in straight public situations, and one of these women said she would be afraid to walk down a half-deserted street with her arm around her lover for fear of being physically attacked. Four women reported difficulty in going out in public with a group of gay women. Seven reported difficulty in going to relatives' homes either alone or with a partner. One woman said, "Visiting my folks with my partner is awkward, but I don't avoid it." Three women said that they had difficulty or found it awkward to have straight friends who did not know they were gay to their home. There were seven other difficult situations mentioned including going to church with partner, business transactions with partner, having lesbian reading material around, having lesbian friends over and fearing being overheard, seeing old friends who didn't know the respondent was gay, discussing "roommate" at work, and having to go to a birth control clinic.

Situations Avoided

Very few women reported avoiding any of the situations given. The mean number of situations avoided was only 1.175 with the maximum number avoided being seven situations. Ten women wrote in responses concerning situations they tried to avoid. Five women indicated that they avoided straight bars. The other responses were varied and included such things as avoiding straight men, showing physical affection in straight public, people hostile to gays, and so forth.

Freedom to Engage in Risk-Taking Behavior

For this measure, seven situations were listed and respondents were asked to indicate which of the behaviors they would feel comfortable engaging in in each situation. Tables B.2-B.8, Appendix B, show the number and percentage of women who would feel free to engage in each behavior in each situation, with the behaviors in each table presented in order of decreasing frequency of selection. It can be seen from these tables that respondents felt consistently more freedom to engage in certain of the behaviors than in others. Freedom to be in close physical proximity, use joint pronouns, and show verbal affection were consistently higher on the list than freedom to discuss the relationship or show physical affection. This was consistent across all situations. In order to determine whether these various behaviors were actually different in terms of how much freedom respondents felt to engage in them, the composite scores were analyzed using t-tests for correlated means for all possible non-redundant pairs. The composite scores were obtained, as explained earlier, by summing behaviors across the first four situations. A radical difference occurred between the first four situations (Appendix B, Tables B.2-B.5) and the last three (Appendix B, Tables B.6-B.8) in terms of the number of behaviors respondents were willing to engage in in each situation. This difference was the basis of the decision to utilize only the first four situations (with relatives, at work or school, in straight public, and with straight friends who don't know respondent is gay) in making up the composite scores. For example, 10 percent of the respondents felt free to show physical affection in the first situation (Appendix B, Table B.2), 15 percent in the next three situations (Appendix B, Tables B.3, B.4 and B.5), and 80 percent, 80 percent, and 89 percent in the last three situations, respectively (Appendix B, Tables B.6, B.7, and B.8). Descriptive statistics for each of the composite scores are presented in Table 4.6.

When this set of composite scores is examined, it can be seen that across the four situations used, the two behaviors respondents most frequently felt free to engage in were: 1) the use of joint pronouns such as "we," "our," and "ours" ($\overline{X}$ = 1.649), and 2) those behaviors involved in maintaining close physical proximity, sitting or standing together, moving around together, and the like ($\overline{X}$ = 1.895). There was no significant difference between these two behaviors, but

TABLE 4.6

Freedom to Engage in Risk-taking Behavior
across Four Situations*

Behavior	Mean	Standard Deviation	Variance
Discuss relationship (1)**	.561	.98	.96
Show physical affection (1)	.614	1.08	1.17
Show verbal affection (2)	.965	1.41	2.00
Use nicknames, terms of endearment (2)	.895	1.30	1.70
Interact as a couple (2)	.930	1.16	1.35
Use joint pronouns (3)	1.649	1.52	2.30
Be in close physical proximity (3)	1.895	1.57	2.45

*With relatives, at work or school, in straight public, and with straight friends who don't know respondent is gay.
**Behaviors followed by the same number do not differ significantly from each other but do differ significantly from all other behaviors.
Source: Compiled by the author.

these two behaviors were engaged in significantly more often than the other behaviors. There were no significant differences among the following behaviors: display of verbal affection ($\overline{X}$ = .965), use of nicknames, terms of endearment ($\overline{X}$ = .895), and interaction as a couple ($\overline{X}$ = .930). The two types of behavior respondents felt least free to engage in were discussing their personal relationship ($\overline{X}$ = .561) and showing physical affection ($\overline{X}$ = .614). These two behaviors did not differ significantly from each other although both differed significantly from all other behaviors.

Three "sets" of behaviors can thus be distinguished on the basis of the freedom respondents felt to engage in them in the four situations considered. Respondents felt most free to be in close physical proximity and to use joint pronouns; they felt least free in all situations to show physical affection and discuss personal relationships. Showing verbal affection, using nicknames or terms of endearment, and acting as a couple fell in between these two extremes in terms of how much freedom respondents felt to engage in these.

A second set of scores was composed for each situation, thus giving two composite scores: one for behaviors and one for situations. As with the behavioral composite score, comparisons were run among the means of all nonredundant pairs of situational scores using a t-test for correlated means. The descriptive data on the composite scores are presented in Table 4.7. Responses in four of the seven situations did not significantly differ. There was no difference found in the freedom respondents felt to engage in all behaviors with relatives ($\overline{X}$ = 1.78), at work or school ($\overline{X}$ = 1.67), in public ($\overline{X}$ = 2.40), or with straight friends who don't know respondent is gay ($\overline{X}$ = 1.85). These four situations differed significantly from the other three. Two of the remaining situations also did not differ significantly from each other, however. There was no difference found in number of behaviors respondents felt free to engage in at a gay bar ($\overline{X}$ = 6.21) or with closest gay friends ($\overline{X}$ = 6.37). One situation fell between these two extremes. Respondents felt significantly less freedom with friends who knew they were gay than with other gay people ($\overline{X}$ = 3.91) and significantly more freedom than with straight friends who didn't know, in public, at work or school, or with relatives.

Passing Behavior

Responses to the 15 items chosen as indicators of passing behavior were not analyzed separately; however, Appendix B, Table B.9 shows the number and percentage of respondents who indicated that they had engaged in each of the behaviors. There were only two

TABLE 4.7

Freedom to Engage in Seven Behaviors
across Seven Situations

Situation	Mean Number of Behaviors	Standard Deviation	Variance
Visiting relatives (1)*	1.78	2.02	4.09
At work or school (1)	1.67	2.34	5.50
In "straight" public (1)	2.40	2.46	6.06
With straight friends who don't know respondent is gay (1)	1.85	2.22	4.94
With straight friends who know respondent is gay (2)	3.91	2.79	7.76
At a gay bar or party (3)	6.21	1.67	2.78
With closest gay friends (3)	6.37	1.60	2.55

*Situations followed by the same number do not differ significantly in
  difficulty but do differ significantly from all other situations in number of behaviors respondents felt free to engage in.
Source: Compiled by the author.

behaviors engaged in by a majority of respondents. Approximately
three-quarters of the respondents introduced a lover or partner as
a "friend," a finding which may say as much about the paucity of the
English language in describing relational nuances as about anything
else. A large majority (67 percent; N = 54) also indicated that they
avoided talking about their living situation. There were two behaviors
that about one-third of the respondents had engaged in. Forty percent (N = 32) reported that they had pretended to date a man. One-
third of the sample (N = 27) had used "he" instead of "she" to refer
to a female lover. Other behaviors were engaged in by fewer than
one-third of the sample. Four women actually married in order to
avoid being identified as lesbian. A sum score of the total number
of behaviors engaged in by each individual was used as the actual
measure of passing behavior. The mean number of such behaviors
was 3.64, although some individuals checked as many as nine.

Other Measures

Others' Knowledge

Respondents were given a list of individuals and groups of individuals and asked to indicate, first, which of these individuals they thought knew they were gay and second, which of these individuals they were sure knew they were gay because they had either told them or discussed it with them.

The mean number of individuals that respondents felt sure knew was 3.54; the mean number that respondents thought knew was 2.19. For both measures, women were more likely to know or be expected to know than were men (Appendix B, Tables B.10 and B.11). For example, women at work were more likely to be expected to know (N = 21) than were men at work (N = 14); mothers were more likely to be expected to know (N = 15) than fathers (N = 8). Respondents' best straight woman friend was more likely to know (N = 45) than respondents' best male friend (N = 31); women at work were more likely to know (N = 30) than men at work (N = 19); and mothers were more likely to know (N = 30) than fathers (N = 20).

One of the most interesting things about these findings is that in all but three cases (relatives, neighbors, and children), the number of individuals who actually knew the respondent was gay was larger than the number whom respondents only thought knew. The women in this sample seemed likely to tell those who might identify them as lesbian, particularly if those people were women, and particularly when they were close (for example, best female friend, best male friend, siblings, women at work, mothers, and most female friends have each been told by at least one-third of the sample). However, the women in the sample cannot be said to have "come out" in general, as only 20 percent of the sample (N = 16) felt that almost everyone they knew was aware that they were lesbian.

Social Contact with Straight People

The great majority of those respondents who were working (94 percent) reported that at least half the people they worked with were straight. Twenty-eight percent of the sample reported that they worked with all straight people, and only four individuals reported working in an all gay setting. Respondents seem to have fairly high social contact with straight people. About 68 percent of the respondents reported having social contact with straight people at least once a month, while 30 percent saw straight people socially as frequently as twice a week (Table 4.8). Responses to open-ended

TABLE 4.8

Frequency of Social Contact with Straight People

Frequency of Contact	N	Percent
At least twice a week	24	30
At least once a week	15	19
At least twice a month	7	9
At least once a month	8	10
Less often than once a month	26	32

Source: Compiled by the author.

questions make it seem likely that these contacts were with individuals who knew that the respondent was gay rather than being with straights who did not know.

Relationships with Other Lesbian Women

The great majority (80 percent) of women in the sample were currently involved with a lover or partner and 67 percent of these were living together. These women therefore had contact with at least one other lesbian woman—their partner—on a fairly frequent basis. As might be expected, social contact with other lesbian women was very high. Sixty-five percent of the respondents had contact with other women at least twice a week, and almost 99 percent of the respondents saw other gay women at least once a month on the average.

Although social contact with other women besides the partner was high, this contact apparently did not take place primarily in bars for these women. Only about 10 percent of the sample reported going to a gay bar as often as twice a week, which means that at least 55 percent of the sample were meeting other lesbian women under other social circumstances. About 40 percent of the women in the sample said that they went to a gay bar as infrequently as twice a year or less, and 17 percent of the sample went less often than once a year.

Attitudes toward Being Lesbian

Respondents were asked to indicate whether or not they liked being lesbian using a 5-point scale (Never = 1; Almost always = 5).

TABLE 4.9

Extent to Which Respondents Liked Being Lesbian

Response (Scale Score)		N	Percent
Never	(1)	0	0
Seldom	(2)	1	1
Sometimes	(3)	6	7
Often	(4)	10	12
Almost always	(5)	64	79

Mean = 4.69
S.D. = .66
Variance = .44
Source: Compiled by the author.

The response was an overwhelmingly favorable one (Table 4.9). No individuals checked the "Never" response, while 79 percent of the sample (N = 64) checked "Almost always." Several women even went so far as to cross out the "Almost" part of the response, thus indicating that they "Always" liked being lesbian. The mean response was 4.69 on a 5-point scale.

Respondents were also asked to indicate to what extent they felt that being lesbian was a choice, as opposed to being something they couldn't help. While the majority of the sample (56 percent) felt that it was entirely their choice, a large proportion (44 percent) felt that at least part of being lesbian was something they couldn't help (Table 4.10). On a 5-point scale (1 = Not at all my choice; 5 = Entirely my choice), the mean response was 4.36.

Finally, there were a number of possible advantages to having relationships with women as opposed to relationships with men which were listed. Respondents were asked to rate each of these in terms of its importance to them using a 5-point scale (1 = Very important; 5 = Not at all important). Of the nine items listed, the three items receiving the highest mean ratings were: "Better communication with a woman than with a man" ($\bar{X}$ = 1.30), "More emotional support from partner" ($\bar{X}$ = 1.40), and "Greater sexual compatibility" ($\bar{X}$ = 1.45). There were no significant differences among the mean ratings for these three scores. Table 4.11 shows the response to each item. No item received a mean rating of less than 3.0 (Somewhat important).

TABLE 4.10

Extent to Which Respondents Felt That
Being Lesbian Was Their Choice

Response (Scale Score)		N	Percent
Not at all	(1)	2	3
Very little	(2)	1	1
Partly	(3)	7	9
Mostly	(4)	24	31
Entirely	(5)	43	56

Mean = 4.36
S.D. = .90
Variance = .80
Source: Compiled by the author.

The two items receiving the lowest ratings were: "Shared responsibility for traditionally feminine tasks" ($\bar{X}$ = 2.76) and "Shared responsibility for traditionally masculine tasks ($\bar{X}$ = 2.86). There was no significant difference between these two means, although both were significantly different from all other means for other items. Respondents were given the opportunity to write in alternative items, but very few did so.

HYPOTHESES

Hypothesis IA

This hypothesis stated that the more a woman felt she could be identified as a lesbian and the more concerned she was about being so identified, the more difficulty she would report in various social situations involving straight people. This hypothesis was partially substantiated on all three independent measures.

Measure 1

A pearson correlation was run between Measure 1 (how often respondent felt she could be identified as lesbian) and the individual items in Question 33 (Appendix A) as well as on the composite scores (mean difficulty and number of difficult items). The results are shown

TABLE 4.11

Perceived Importance of Advantages to Having
Relationships with Women Rather Than with Men*

Advantage	Mean	Standard Deviation	Variance
Better communication with a woman than with a man (1)**	1.32	.81	.66
More emotional support from partner (1, 2)	1.42	.79	.62
Greater sexual compatibility (1, 2)	1.52	.98	.96
Greater flexibility in role expectations (2, 3)	1.54	1.07	1.14
Freedom from male dominance (3, 4)	1.79	1.21	1.46
Freedom from traditional woman's role (4)	1.87	1.27	1.61
Greater acceptance of traditionally nonfeminine behavior (5)	2.08	1.38	1.90
Shared responsibility for traditionally feminine tasks (5)	2.76	1.42	2.02
Shared responsibility for traditionally masculine tasks (5)	2.86	1.38	1.90

*Using a 5-point scale where 1 = very important; 5 = not at all
important.
**Items followed by the same number do not differ significantly.
Source: Compiled by the author.

in Table 4.12. Only three of the individual items showed a significant correlation with this measure. The more a woman thought others could tell she was gay, the more difficulty she felt she would have going to a straight party alone ($r = -.37$, $p < .001$); the more difficulty she felt she would have going to a straight party with her partner ($r = -.23$, $p < .03$); and the more difficulty she felt she would have going to a nice restaurant with her partner ($r = -.21$, $p < .04$). Measure 1 also showed a significant correlation with the number of items an individual marked as at least somewhat difficult ($r = .21$, $p < .05$), but there was no correlation with mean difficulty.

Measure 2

Pearson correlations were run between Measure 2 and the dependent variables. This measure correlated highly with six of the individual items on the dependent variable and with both of the composite scores (Table 4.13). The more a woman thought about being identified as gay when around straight people, the more difficulty she expected in various social situations: going to a straight party alone ($r = -.28$, $p < .007$), going to a straight party with a partner ($r = -.25$, $p < .02$), going to a nice restaurant with a partner ($r = -.33$, $p < .002$), having a partner phone frequently at work ($r = -.27$, $p < .03$), having straight friends to her home ($r = -.38$, $p < .001$), and having relatives to her home ($r = -.29$, $p < .005$) were all seen as more difficult. Women who were concerned about being identified

TABLE 4.12

Relationship between Self-Perceived Visibility
and Difficulty in Social Situations

Dependent Variable	r	r^2	p
Going to a straight party alone	-.37	.14	.001
Going to a straight party with partner	-.23	.05	.03
Going to a nice restaurant with partner	-.21	.04	.04
Number of difficult items	.21	.04	.05

Source: Compiled by the author.

TABLE 4.13

Relationship between Thinking about Being Identified,
Number of Items Leading to Visibility, and
Difficulty in Social Situations

Thinking about Being Identified (Measure 2) with:	r	r^2	p
Going to a straight party alone	-.28	.08	.007
Going to a straight party with partner	-.25	.06	.02
Going to a nice restaurant with partner	-.33	.11	.002
Having partner phone frequently at work	-.27	.07	.03
Having straight friends to home	-.38	.14	.001
Having relatives to home	-.29	.08	.005
Number of Items Leading to Visibility (Measure 3) with:	r	r^2	p
Going to a straight party alone	-.38	.14	.001

Source: Compiled by the author.

also had significantly greater perceptions of difficulty in social situations as reflected by mean difficulty scores ($r = .26$, $p < .02$) and by
number of difficult items ($r = .27$, $p < .007$).

Measure 3

Pearson correlations were run between Measure 3 and the
dependent measures of difficulty in social situations. Only one
individual item was significant: the greater the number of things a
woman felt could tip others off that she was gay, the more difficulty
she felt she would have going to a straight party alone ($r = -.38$,
$p < .001$). None of the correlations of this measure with the composite scores were significant.

Hypothesis IB

This hypothesis stated that the more a woman felt she could
be identified as a lesbian and the more concerned she was about being
so identified, the more social situations which involved straight people
she would avoid. This hypothesis was not substantiated. There were
no significant correlations between any of the measures and the number of situations avoided. It is believed that the reason for this is
most probably the extremely low number of situations women said
they avoided and the consequently low variance on this variable.

Hypothesis IC

This hypothesis stated that the more a woman felt she could
be identified as a lesbian and the more concerned she was about being
so identified, the greater the number of behaviors she would engage
in around straight people in order to avoid being identified as lesbian.
This hypothesis was not substantiated for Measures 1 and 3, but was
substantiated for Measure 2. A pearson correlation was run between
Measure 2 and the total number of items checked as ways women have
attempted to avoid being identified as lesbian. There was a significant correlation ($r = .23$, $r^2 = .05$, $p < .02$) between the extent to
which an individual thought about being identified and the number of
ways she tried to avoid being identified.

Hypothesis ID

This hypothesis stated that the more a woman felt she could be
identified as a lesbian and the more concerned she was about being
so identified, the fewer risk-taking behaviors which might cause her
to be identified as a lesbian she would engage in around straight
people. This hypothesis was substantiated for Measure 3, but not
for Measures 1 and 2. Significant results were obtained for Measures
1 and 2, but they were in a direction opposite from that predicted.

Measure 1

A significant correlation was found between the extent to which
a respondent felt she could be identified as a lesbian and the number
of behaviors she felt free to engage in in the company of work or
school associates ($r = .35$, $p < .002$). Significant correlations were
also found between Measure 1 and the extent to which a woman felt
free to show physical affection across situations ($r = .43$, $p < .001$),

the extent to which she felt free to show verbal affection across situations ($r = .30$, $p < .01$), and the extent to which she felt free to use terms of endearment with her partner across situations ($r = .24$, $p < .04$). In all instances, the more a woman thought she could be identified, the greater freedom she felt to engage in these behaviors (Table 4.14).

Measure 2

This measure correlated negatively with a number of items and was the only one of the three to substantiate the hypothesis. The more individuals reported thinking about whether straights knew they were gay, the less freedom they felt in two situations: in straight public ($r = -.23$, $p < .02$) and when visited by straight friends who didn't know they were gay ($r = -.30$, $p < .005$). This measure was also highly correlated with five of the seven different behaviors summed across situations. The more an individual thought about whether straights knew she was gay, the less freedom she felt to use nicknames or terms of endearment ($r = -.23$, $p < .04$), to discuss the relationship ($r = -.24$, $p < .04$), to interact on a personal level ($r = -.24$, $p < .04$), to use joint pronouns when discussing experiences

TABLE 4.14

Relationship between Self-Perceived Visibility
and Freedom to Engage in Risk-Taking Behaviors

Dependent Variable	r	r^2	p
Number of behaviors engaged in in company of work or school associates	.35	.12	.002
Freedom to show physical affection across situations	.43	.18	.001
Freedom to show verbal affection across situations	.30	.09	.01
Freedom to use terms of endearment across situations	.24	.06	.04

Source: Compiled by the author.

TABLE 4.15

Relationship between Thinking about Visibility and
Freedom to Engage in Risk-Taking Behaviors

Dependent Variable	r	r^2	p
Number of behaviors engaged in in straight public	-.23	.05	.02
Number of behaviors engaged in when visited by straight friends who don't know respondent is gay	-.30	.09	.005
Freedom to use nicknames, terms of endearment across situations	-.23	.05	.04
Freedom to discuss the relationship across situations	-.24	.06	.04
Freedom to interact on a personal level	-.24	.06	.04
Freedom to use joint pronouns across situations	-.39	.15	.001
Freedom to be in close physical proximity	-.25	.06	.03

Source: Compiled by the author.

and the like ($r = -.39$, $p < .001$), and to be in close physical proximity
($r = -.25$, $p < .03$) (Table 4.15).

Measure 3

Significant correlations occurred between Measure 3 and two
situations: with relatives ($r = .22$, $p < .03$) and in the company of
straight friends who knew the respondent was gay ($r = .19$, $p < .05$).
A significant correlation was also found between Measure 3 and freedom to show verbal affection across situations ($r = .28$, $p < .02$).
In all instances, the more items a woman felt could tip straights off
that she was gay, the more likely she was to feel free to engage in
these behaviors.

Hypothesis IIA

This hypothesis stated that the more heterosexual experiences a woman had, the less difficulty she would report in various social situations involving straight people. This hypothesis was not substantiated for either the Kinsey scale or for marital status. The only significant result obtained was the finding that women who had been married experienced significantly less difficulty going to a straight party alone than did women who had not been married ($t = -2.04$, $df = 75$, $p < .04$).

Hypothesis IIB

This hypothesis stated that the more heterosexual experience a woman had, the fewer the number of social situations involving straight people she would avoid. This hypothesis was not substantiated for either of the independent measures.

Hypothesis IIC

The hypothesis stated that the more heterosexual experiences a woman had, the fewer behaviors she would engage in around straight people in order to avoid being identified as lesbian. This hypothesis was not substantiated for either of the independent measures.

Hypothesis IID

This hypothesis stated that the more heterosexual experience a woman had, the more risk-taking behaviors which might cause her to be identified as a lesbian she would feel free to engage in around straight people. This hypothesis was not substantiated for either of the independent measures.

5

DISCUSSION AND

CONCLUSIONS

SECONDARY DEVIANCE

In sociological terms, most of the women in the study can be said to be secondary deviants, not necessarily because of having been labeled by others, but because they are self-labeled as lesbians, they are obviously aware of possible ostracism, and they are essentially committed to a lesbian life style. Many are women who organize a large part of their lives around the fact of sexual preference. This is a group of women who, for the most part, like being lesbian, find a number of advantages to relationships with women, and have frequent, though rarely exclusive, contacts with members of the gay community. They are women over half of whom identify being lesbian as an important part of their lives:

> It is my whole life. I can be myself. I can grow.
> I don't have to waste energy on men (emotional
> energy). I can put all of my energy where it will
> ultimately be returned to me.*

> It is extremely important to me that I am a lesbian
> and a feminist. . . . The lesbian consciousness that
> I share with my lover and a few lesbian friends, and
> via their writings with other women, informs my
> whole life—particularly the way I view the world.

---

*Quotes in this section are taken from the open-ended questions on the questionnaire unless otherwise specified.

It affects the way I see both the general and the particular. It is the reassertion of the primacy of women and the nurturing, life-giving qualities they have. It is hard to describe, but it provides an organizing principle to my life and links me in a way with all women everywhere who have loved women. It's similar to a religion.

It is very important in terms of the philosophical and practical orientation I have toward living—mainly in terms of a . . . woman-centeredness and concern with considering women's issues, ideas, opinions while not paying much attention to the male world. On the other hand, my being a lesbian is less important than my being the person I am and am becoming—in terms of how I actually live my life, it seems less central in my identity than it did when I first came out.

When I 'came out' I was making a political choice of great importance. I was being gay in a closeted way for years—loving women can be simple, but now I consider it vital in a political-strategy sense to identify myself as lesbian and consciously revolutionize me and the culture I'm in. I'm truly proud of me in many ways including the woman I love and my efforts in developing a woman-culture. It was time for me to quit buying the many forms of oppression and step forward. In this sense the label lesbian is vital. (Italics added)

Several women pointed out very clearly the role of society in making lesbianism important for them:

Being gay is to me quite normal, healthy—I can't say whether or not it is a large or small part of my life— it is 'being me'—totally integrated, together, settled, satisfied with what I am. It is not something I flaunt or push or fight about. I cannot say it is irrelevant because society does not consider it so (italics added); it is very important, largely so only because I wish for society in general to accept all human beings—be they heterosexual or homosexual . . . I desire (also want to help it to become a reality) for all gay people to be considered and treated as human beings not 'queers,' 'deviants,' 'character disorders,' or what have you—'frieks?' (sic).

(Being gay) is pretty major. Mostly because it's so
obvious to me that I'm considered different or deviant
or interesting because of it. And also because my
emotional and sexual life and my whole political outlook
have changed since I came out. It would be nice if it
were slightly less 'relevant.'

I think being gay is a large part of and is very important to my life. We can't deny our sexuality, and it is
so much a part of us we can't separate ourselves from
it. In the straight world, it is all taken for granted,
in media, and so on. In the gay world, a lot of things
made me aware of my sexuality being so strong and all
of me—not just a little bit of me.

Being gay is important to me and is made even more
so by the reactions of the 'straight society' which sur-
rounds me. I'm am (sic) constantly aware of it and
spend most of my nonworking hours in a gay subculture.
This is where I am most comfortable and at ease.

When I am with other gay people the issue seems mild
or commonplace. In that context, the issue plays a
small part in my life. When I am out in public, at work,
at school, the issue seems almost (to me) comparable
to an underground war faction. I feel like a partisan.

Although these are women who have high contact with the gay
community and find it important, they are also women who, for the
most part, work with predominantly straight individuals and have
social contacts with straight people at least once a month. All in all,
this is a group of women who are committed to a gay life style and
yet whose members are involved to some extent in the straight world;
these are women who move back and forth from gay to straight worlds
rather consistently and have commitments and ties in each.

MANAGEMENT AND PASSING

Visibility

While these are women who seem to identify closely with a
lesbian life style, they do not consider themselves to be identifiable
as lesbians except, perhaps, when in the company of other gay women.

Fewer than one-fourth of them can be said to have "come out" to most of the people they know. They don't seem to think that there are many physical characteristics which could tip others off to the fact of their gayness. The two most frequently indicated items which they did feel could tip others off, "single status" and "interests," can be either disguised or accounted for if the individual so chooses. These women also did not seem to worry about being identified as lesbian to any great extent when around straight people. It should be noted, however, that while the majority of women in the sample do not seem to be extensively concerned with being identified, there is a minority of women who are concerned (although these are not necessarily the ones who felt most identifiable) and as the data indicate, these are the women who seem to undertake the most management.

Because the women in this sample are involved in a gay life style, don't feel highly visible, and have both work and social contacts with straight people, they are precisely the kind of people whom one might expect to be able to pass and to have a stake in trying to do so. The basic assumption of this study was that, as Garfinkel (1967) has suggested, for individuals who are trying to pass, routine day-to-day activities can be "specifically and chronically problematic." It was felt that such activities would be more problematic the more visible an individual felt herself to be.

In terms of the independent variables, visibility was measured in three ways (Measures 1-3): how often a woman thought she could be identified as lesbian (Measure 1); how often she thought about being identified as a lesbian when in the company of straight people (Measure 2); and how many things about her could tip straights off (Measure 3). The relationship of these three independent variables to the dependent variables indicated that what was important in making deviance problematic for the respondents was not how visible a woman thought she was per se, but whether or not she was concerned about being visible when around straights. It seemed likely that perhaps those who were concerned about being visible were so concerned because they felt basically more identifiable. This was not necessarily the case, however, as the low correlations among the three independent measures demonstrated. This finding, along with the differential effects of these three measures on the dependent variables, suggests that the measures are getting at very different aspects of visibility.

Dependent Variables

Situational Difficulty

The four dependent variables also provide some interesting information. On the measure of situational difficulty, a number of situations differed significantly in perceived difficulty. Having relatives to one's home, going alone to a straight party, and going to a straight party with one's partner all are significantly more difficult than other situations and do not differ from each other in difficulty. It is not surprising that these situations should be considered more difficult than others, for each carries strong social implications about both sexual and sex-role behavior. Straight parties obviously carry implications for appropriate behavior toward members of the opposite sex. If a woman comes alone to such a function, she is likely to be considered available. If she is not available and makes this known, then she is in the difficult position of having to explain why she is not available. If she acts as though she were available, she may find herself in an awkward situation. Most parties suggest, by definition, that relationships will be developed or renewed or deepened in some way. Straight parties operate on the assumption that such relationships will have a heterosexual base. The connotations of assumed heterosexuality, single status (in heterosexual terms), and presence at a straight party or function can definitely make things hard. As one woman stated:

(It's difficult for me) generally being around straight men or in a situation in which I could be considered available for straight men to pick up. I try to avoid straight bars and clubs and parties unless there are just close straight friends there who know I'm a lesbian.

And another woman commented:

My age precludes my having to have a male partner at social functions though surprisingly there are still people wanting to 'fix me up' with some guy—and still the question 'Why isn't a nice girl like you married?'

Another problem may be that at straight parties (as at most social functions), one is expected to share more of oneself than one shares at the office. One is expected to be social. For many gay women, this kind of expectation can be awkward. At a party, it may mean too many relationships to be negotiated, too much to be explained or avoided, too many difficult questions to answer, too much to hide or lie about. This may be particularly (though certainly not exclusively) true where men are concerned:

> Often I have met men whom I have considered fascinating
> people. Something in me resists cultivating friendships
> with such men—a fear of being belittled should I be
> 'found out' as gay. I find this to be a regressive and
> uncomfortable condition, but invariably find myself
> cutting short such friendships.

For most women in the study, the problem of straight parties did not seem to be one that came up frequently except, perhaps, at work. Many women said that they avoided parties which were predominantly straight or in which the straight people did not know they were gay.

Going to a straight party with one's partner probably presents different problems from going alone. Although it was rated as a difficult situation, no one commented on this particular situation in the open-ended questions. It seemed likely that unless the couple involved was either up-front about being lesbian or could reasonably be expected to come to a party independent of each other (for example, in the instance in which partners may work in the same setting), going to such a party would be highly problematic for everyone involved and was thus probably avoided in most instances.

Having relatives to one's home (or going to relatives' homes) seemed to be a universally difficult problem. Even those women who said that they really had no management problems frequently mentioned parents as the one hitch in an otherwise comfortable life style. Although few people went into detail in describing problems with relatives in the open-ended questions, personal conversations with lesbian women brought out a number of anecdotes, horror stories, and traumatic situations. While going out into the straight world does certainly create management problems of various sorts, relatives may be an even more complex issue. It is frequently of concern to parents whom their daughter dates, how often she dates, when and if she expects to get married, and how soon they can expect not only a son-in-law, but grandchildren. While these issues may be handled with reasonable finesse over the phone, the presence of relatives in one's home may call for extreme measures. Women reported having to remove books on lesbianism and homosexuality from bookshelves, take down posters, alter sleeping arrangements, warn friends, invent boyfriends, and occasionally dispose of lovers for the duration of the visit. Perhaps the worst part is the strain of having to be less than honest with members of one's family and of expecting and sometimes suffering rejection if they become aware of one's sexual preference. One woman commented, for example, that when "my mother was discussing grandchildren . . . (she) referred to my brother and sister. I was overlooked. I was nonexistent."

For the most part, even though these three situations were seen as more difficult than others, the general impression created by the respondents was that being gay was not considered highly problematic. Responses to the open-ended questions showed that the specific types of situations given in this question, as well as the use of the term "difficult," may have resulted in the questionnaire failing to get at the most problematic areas. Responses to several of the open-ended questions made it seem likely that the women in this study didn't think of the ordinary situations in their lives as being difficult to any great extent. These women were not passively waiting to be mistreated by nondeviants; they were not, in the manner of Garfinkel's subject, caught in a morass of problematic situations. They organized their lives, as much as possible, so that they avoided being in situations which were potentially difficult or which they were likely to find uncomfortable. Those situations (for example, with relatives or at work) where the straight world impinged unavoidably did not seem to be viewed as difficult as much as they were viewed as situations calling for an unpleasant, but unavoidable, amount of subterfuge. For example, in response to the question "What are the most negative aspects to being a gay woman, in your experience," these were a few of the answers:

> Not being able to express yourself honestly at times
> as a heterosexual person could.

> 1) being reticent to tell a close heterosexual friend the
> same things she talks about to me in her relationship.
> I feel like I'm cheating them out of an intimate relation-
> ship and not giving on my part; 2) looking single and the
> sub rosa connotations of that; 3) being uncomfortable
> when asked 'you're a good looking girl, why haven't
> you gotten married?' I've no good smart come back
> for all that which the question implies.

> Being separated from straight society: like not being
> able to say at work that Judy is my lover. Knowing
> my credibility will be shot as soon as other people
> know I'm gay.

And in response to a question concerning the type of day-to-day management which was undertaken, another woman said:

> It's most painful to want to tell someone (straight male
> or female) I'm gay but not to jeopardize job or work
> relationships. Don't want to be token deviant! But
> want to come out—self-respect and want closer relation-
> ship with person.

What these women are really talking about are not situations
as much as relationships; situations in which "parties to a transaction have mutually recognized parts to play in the transaction."
For these women, it is not the situation or the transaction per se
which is difficult, but rather the part that they are being called upon
to play vis-a-vis straight people, and the possible interpretation of
themselves based on the way the part is played. For example, one
woman said:

> You have to cut off so much personal information that
> would otherwise be shared with straight friends.
> Makes you appear as a shallow, unemotional person.

Being gay, in this instance, can affect the way others see her (or at
least the way she believes they see her). The options here are both
unpleasant: to be straightforward about one's sexual preference and
risk the possible negative consequences or to continue to hide and
risk being seen as shallow or unemotional. This type of hiding can
also affect one's perception of oneself. As one woman commented:

> (Being gay) limits my life because it has made me
> dishonest in basic up-front relationships with straight
> people; it has made me fearful of exposure; it has made
> me a devious person. I don't feel I would be these
> ways otherwise.

And another woman's remarks pointed up the relationship between
the necessity felt for passing and self-acceptance:

> Since quitting my job as a school teacher and discussing
> my homosexuality with my mother, I no longer feel the
> need to hide the fact that I am gay. . . . Quitting my
> job has helped me tremendously in accepting myself as
> a homosexual. When you have to hide an aspect of your
> life in order to protect a job, it's hard to feel good
> about that particular aspect of your life.

In sum, it appears that, with the reference to specific difficult situations, the difficulty is not so much in the situations themselves as in

the relationships which women may be involved in and in self-interpretation and/or expected interpretations of others within those relationships.

Risk-Taking Behaviors

On the measure which asked respondents to indicate which behaviors they would engage in in a variety of situations, there were significant situational differences. While it may seem obvious that women would be more comfortable engaging in various behaviors in different situational contexts, there has been (to the author's knowledge) no substantiation of that assumption until now. For this sample, at least, the major differences were among three types of situations: 1) those where people did not know the respondent was gay (for example, in public or with straight friends who don't know) or where there might be some threat associated with "overt" behavior (for example, at work or with relatives); 2) those situations involving straight friends who did know the respondent was lesbian; and 3) those involving gay people.

An interesting finding is that respondents felt freer with straight friends who knew they were gay than with those who didn't, but significantly less free than with gay friends. It is logical to assume that the greatest amount of management would occur in preventing people from finding out that one is lesbian, but obviously some type of management occurs even after the need to pass no longer exists. To follow a common-sense approach, it appears that there is some sort of continuum of management which covers a variety of situations and the behaviors acceptable in each. It was pointed out earlier that most individuals have learned the same set of behaviors necessary to function as normal within societal boundaries. It seems likely that as long as the so-called deviant remains within these boundaries (in this case, those applying to straight society), the prevailing set of rules for interaction are those of the dominant group. Thus, the awareness of the respondent's lesbianism on the part of straights is not taken by the lesbian woman as license for moving from straight to gay rules. It is certainly the case that the presence of even one straight individual in a group of gays is frequently sufficient to cause all present to conform to straight society's rules for appropriate behavior among members of the same sex. The small number of answers to open-ended questions which related to this issue indicated that lesbian women felt that just because others knew about their lesbianism did not mean that they were comfortable with manifestations of it. Correctly or incorrectly, the women in this study obviously discriminated clearly among situations involving those who knew about and shared their sexual preference and those who knew about but did not share it. Although the questions about respondents' behavior referred to what they did in the presence of friends who knew, a number of the open-ended answers related specifically to relatives. It is not known what differences there may be between the reactions of and to relatives versus friends, but it is obvious from the three responses quoted below that telling relatives can create complex management situations.

> I don't (hide the fact that I'm gay) and never have with close friends though I never discuss or act upon these things around my parents. They accept both of us, always invite us both to dinner, and so on. There's an unspoken agreement to not speak about it. If ever my friend can't come they always seem surprised and disappointed.

> (It has been difficult) dealing with the feelings my mother had about my being gay. I hated to disappoint what she might have wanted me to be although by the time it was obvious she was too ill to have the energy to deal with it further. It was a breach in an otherwise very close relationship.

> I don't think about being gay except around my parents. They know I'm gay and they accept it, yet emotionally it is hard for them to accept it. So I avoid the subject even though I have talked about it. They would rather talk about it than actually see the reality of it, that is, bringing my lover to their house. (Italics added)

In terms of specific behaviors which respondents felt free to engage in within the four situations perceived as most restrictive, the differences found were not really surprising, except perhaps for the finding that respondents were as unwilling to discuss their personal relationships as they were to engage in physical affection in the presence of straight people.

Avoiding Identification

The types of behaviors that women reported having engaged in or avoided in order to keep from being identified as lesbian give some idea of the variety of things lesbian women may do to protect themselves. While only two of these behaviors were checked by the majority of women (introducing one's lover as a friend and avoiding talking about one's living situation), at least a quarter of the sample have

engaged in a number of the other behaviors at one time or another.
It is amazing to the author that the women in the sample were as
(relatively) uncomplaining as they were when one realizes that many
of them have felt it necessary at one time or another to hide parts of
their lives in various ways which cover the gamut from using "he"
instead of "she" to refer to one's lover to actually getting married.
While many of the behaviors may not have taken place in any continu-
ous fashion, or may be necessary only with certain people or in certain places, still the necessity for hiding one's life in these ways
cannot help but be unpleasant.

The main impression which is gathered from these data is the
extent to which, as Garfinkel found, management seems to consist
of small things; frequently, it is an avoidance of behaviors or actions
which heterosexuals might take very much for granted. These women
do not undergo extraordinary daily crises, as far as one can tell;
they are not overwhelmed by the magnitude of their public and private
behavioral discrepancies; they are not schizoid or even highly har-
assed. Their energy is expended, insofar as they expend energy on
management at all, on small-scale, daily efforts: avoiding displays
of physical or verbal affection, avoiding the use of nicknames or
terms of endearment, altering personal pronouns, keeping conversations and relationships on safe ground. These women, if they wish
to pass, seem to believe that they must primarily avoid revealing to
others the nature and extent of their feelings for and about a woman
(or women). It was originally anticipated that lesbian women would
be actively attempting to convey an image of straightness. It appears,
however, that the major efforts these women make are not to be
intrusively or obviously lesbian. The types of behaviors mentioned
above must be avoided precisely because in heterosexual couples
they are so clearly an indication of involvement and intimacy; they
are so much a part and parcel of many relationships and are so easily
and unthinkingly carried over into nonprivate, social situations: the
references to one's husband's or wife's behavior; to one's vacations,
weekends, evenings, experiences; the expression of fondness or
interest when talking about someone loved; the frequency with which
one may mention a lover or partner; and so forth. Several women
mentioned the difficulty of this general type of restriction:

> Having to hide being gay, both to the public, family and
> friends (is difficult). (So is) not being able to openly
> express love or emotion.

> (It's hard) not being able to express yourself honestly
> at times as a heterosexual person could.

> (What's difficult is) lack of freedom to respond openly
> toward your partner and/or to discuss one's personal
> and private happenings and goals when in public, with
> straight people, and in particular, with members of my
> family.

In sum, these are a group of women who do not consider themselves highly visible, do not worry about being identified as lesbian to any great extent, yet who do undertake some degree of management. They are women who, for the most part, hide being lesbian by not talking about their living situations and/or by introducing lovers as friends. Being with relatives, in straight public, at work, and with straight friends who don't know they are gay are all occasions for curtailing a lot of partnership behavior, particularly displays of affection and indications of closeness or intimacy. With straight friends, and presumably family, who know they are gay, these women are more likely to engage in a variety of behaviors than they are with those who don't know, but they still feel significantly less freedom than when with other gay people.

HYPOTHESES

Self-Perceived Visibility

Difficulty in Social Situations

In terms of difficulty in social situations, all three independent measures showed the same thing: in those situations where the independent measures made a difference, greater visibility was associated with greater situational difficulty. However, the independent measure which made the most difference was Measure 2 (thinking about being identified). This measure was related to difficulty in six specific situations as well as two of the composite difficulty scores. All three measures were significantly related to difficulty in going to a straight party and both Measure 1 (likelihood of being identified as lesbian) and Measure 2 were correlated with difficulty in going to a straight party with one's partner and going to a nice restaurant with one's partner. It is suggested that these three items tap a dimension different from that measured by other items—that the difficulty in these situations is related to the basic assumptions of heterosexuality which may underlie all of them.

Both the straight party and the restaurant are situations in which a woman is typically either escorted by a man or in which heterosexuality is the underlying assumption. To be with another woman at a nice restaurant if one is gay <u>and</u> believes oneself to be identifiable may mean that one is more conspicuous than in other settings. So many of the niceties at restaurants include or involve sex-role assumptions: making a reservation, ordering a meal, ordering and tasting the wine, and so forth. Nice restaurants may also have either a stated or assumed dress code which could make some lesbian women uncomfortable, particularly if they are accustomed to a more informal style of dress. Some restaurants or clubs also cater largely or exclusively to couples which may make things awkward. As one woman commented:

> (Being lesbian) does limit life style in a way when it comes to wanting to go 'out on the town' all dressed up, and so on. Can't go to nice places where it's couples only. Gay bars are all right, but neat formal places are too once in a while.

On all measures, going to a straight party alone was the item on which there was the highest correlation between the independent and dependent measures. The fact that straight parties are particularly difficult for those who feel visible again brings up the issue of negotiation of relationships which was discussed earlier. While one may feel identifiable as a lesbian in some contexts without discomfort, the party situation may make the issue of sexuality particularly salient and may thus highlight feelings of deviance. For most women in the study, the issue of straight parties was not one which seemed to come up frequently, except perhaps around work. Many women said that they avoided parties which were predominantly straight unless the straight people included knew they were gay.

What these data seem to be showing is not so much what kinds of situations are actually perceived as difficult, for none were rated as being highly problematic, but rather that there are in fact differences between those women who do and those who don't worry a lot about being identified as lesbian and that there are several specific types of situations in which self-perceived visibility, as well as concern over visibility, can affect one's perception of situational difficulty.

Day-to-Day Management

Similar data are found when we consider the number of ways women attempt to avoid being identified as lesbian. Self-perceived visibility turns out in this instance to be unrelated, but the extent to which one thinks about being identified does affect a number of behaviors. Much of this type of behavioral control seems to take place at work and/or with relatives or friends. Because it was felt that the situations given might not cover the most important contingencies, an open-ended question was asked:

> In your day-to-day life, are there any social situations
> which occur frequently which require management on
> your part to hide the fact that you are gay? If so,
> please describe these situations and how you hide the
> fact that you are a lesbian.

Sixty-two women answered the question and 26 of these (42 percent of those answering; 32 percent of the total) said there were no situations which required management on a day-to-day basis; that means that fewer than half of those in the sample felt that there were problematic daily situations. This is a rather different finding from what was expected.

A number of those who indicated that there were no day-to-day problems attributed this to being involved primarily with women in their daily lives or to restricting social activities to the gay community to a great extent. Most often, and this is not really surprising, the main problematic situations for these women occurred at work, and in almost all instances involved social rather than work-related issues.

> For school activities I am expected to attend, most
> other teachers bring their spouses or boyfriends or
> girlfriends. I feel more comfortable going alone to
> hide the fact that my friend is a woman (I'd rather have
> my friend go, but I can't allow myself this privilege.)

> Teachers and friends always inquiring 'Who are you
> dating now? I hide my lesbianism by saying 'Jim'
> a gay male friend whom I take to school functions.

> The only literal day-to-day social situations which
> I feel need concealing efforts on my part are at work.
> I hide the fact that I am a lesbian at work by not talking
> about my personal life in other than a very superficial
> way. Other less frequent social situations are relating
> to the neighbors and the landlady. I conceal by not
> inviting them into our apartment and by not referring
> to my partner in conversations.

> When the women at work start talking about their
> love lives. On the one hand, I want to tell them how

great loving a woman is, on the other hand I want to
avoid the subject completely.

One woman described a rather unique situation:

> With male clients (for whom I do graphic design) often
> I am 'propositioned'—(this is not offensive to me)—it is
> just 'normal' male behavior and I am attractive to most
> men. . . . I am tempted to disclose my lesbian life style
> to fend men off. This has proven repeatedly to be a
> direct invitation for the man to 'prove' his prowess
> sexually, and to 'show' me I just never found the 'right'
> man! I have since learned to rather deftly keep the
> 'atmosphere' centered on business at hand and to be
> very businesslike with other appointments pending
> which will prohibit time spent 'at play' with the man.
> If I know the man well enough he knows I am gay,
> accepts it, and doesn't become 'pushy.' Also, he is
> not insulted by a turn-down—because he 'understands.'

Other common situations which came up, again most frequently at
work, involved concealing one's personal life either by avoiding talking about it or by pretending that things done as a couple were done
alone:

> In working situations (I) often avoid <u>any</u> discussion of
> my personal life outside of a simple 'I am moving' or
> 'I'm going camping with a friend,' and so on.

> (It's difficult) when casually talking about my weekend
> with the men coworkers and some women coworkers. . . .
> There's a lot of gaps of time unaccounted for in my talk-
> ing about it. I just talk about the acceptable parts—
> 'I went to the beach.' 'I cleaned house,' and so on.

> In talking about the events of the past weekend, I avoid
> discussing my roommate. I also don't openly talk to
> her on the phone at work and feel a little paranoid about
> it when I do.

> (I) don't talk about my love life—refer to 'her' as my
> roommate specially at work where some people do not
> know of our relationship. My family is not in this
> country so when I write to them I just mention her in
> a very light way.

For the most part, the women in the sample seemed to be able to manage these day-to-day situations without their being terribly problematic, although they may be uncomfortable. What is amazing is that these women do not see management as more of a problem than they do. While it may not sound harassing, a moment's thought should indicate how pervasive such forms of management could be and how much daily energy they could require. It is not easy, although it may become automatic, to continually script one's relationships so that large areas of one's personal life are avoided, so that one does not make reference to someone whom one loves and with whom one spends one's private life. For many gay couples, this may be the equivalent of one partner in a marriage feeling compelled to conceal the existence of the other and the importance of shared experiences. It frequently means that, as has been shown, relationships with straights are curtailed, limited, or avoided particularly where there is threat or fear of ostracism or loss of a job.

Risk-Taking Behavior

Some of the most interesting results of the study are connected with Hypothesis ID. As with other dependent variables, women who were concerned about being identified as lesbian were again least likely to engage in risk-taking behaviors. By contrast, those women who perceived themselves as more highly visible were significantly more likely to engage in some kinds of risk-taking behavior than those who considered themselves less visible. What this finding suggests is that some respondents know they are more visible because they act more visible; they try less to conceal themselves. What this may be reflecting is that these women are, for the most part, not engaged in attempting to pass. The correlations between Measures 1 and 3 and between 2 and 3 show that some of those women who are concerned about being identified are the same women who feel visible, but the amount of variance explained is quite small. There appear to be other women who feel that they are visible because they don't try to hide or pass. These may be the women who feel more freedom to engage in risk-taking behavior around straight people. This means that, rather than being causal, the independent variable of visibility as defined by Measures 1 and 3 may really be more concurrent with the dependent measure of risk taking. That is, these women may feel visible because they engage in risk-taking behavior, rather than the other way around. It seems quite likely that the measures of the independent variable were actually not refined enough to differentiate among those women who do not wish to be visible but feel that they are anyway and those who do not attempt to pass and thus feel that they are visible.

When all responses are looked at together, respondents did not differentiate among the first four situations in terms of number of behaviors they would feel free to engage in. There was very low freedom indicated with relatives; at work or school, or in the company of work or school associates; in straight public; and with straight friends who didn't know the respondent was gay. While respondents felt more freedom with straight friends who did know they were gay than in the preceding four types of situations, they felt less free with them than at a gay bar, or party, or with closest gay friends.

When the issue of visibility is introduced, Measure 1 only made a difference in terms of work or school associates, not where relatives, friends, or straight public were concerned. Measure 3 was related to greater freedom with relatives and with straight friends who knew the respondent was gay. This difference in effect of the two independent measures was not predicted and cannot be accounted for given the available data. The one thing which is consistent for these two independent measures is that both show greater self-perceived visibility to be related to greater freedom to engage in risk-taking behavior.

Measure 1 and Measure 3 differ completely from Measure 2. On Measure 2, respondents who thought about being identified felt less freedom to engage in all behaviors in straight public and with friends who didn't know they were gay.

Although the differences in effect of Measures 1 and 3 were not predicted and cannot be accounted for given the available data, the difference between these two measures and Measure 2 may be understandable in the light of concepts discussed earlier. A number of authors (Davis 1961; Emerson 1973; Garfinkel 1967; Glaser and Strauss 1964; Laing, Phillipson, and Lee 1966; and Scheff 1973) point out the _negotiable_ aspect of identities and relationships, particularly as this applies to deviant individuals. Davis (1961) describes the process which occurs in the management of interactions by individuals with "non-self-inflicted social injury, the visible physical handicap." He breaks the process down into three stages:

1) fictional acceptance, 2) the facilitation of reciprocal role-taking around a normalized projection of self, and 3) the institutionalization in the relationship of a definition of self that is normal in its moral dimension, however qualified it may be with respect to its situational contexts (p. 125).

Emerson (1973) talks about the negotiation of "stance" between the deviant and nondeviant and suggests that interactants will frequently take the stance that "nothing unusual is happening" in order to minimize social cost. She also points out that it is not only the nondeviant who is liable to engage in defining such a stance:

> Definitions of reality, such as 'nothing unusual is happening' and 'something unusual is happening,' are negotiated. Ambiguity allows more scope for negotiations. Ambiguity is produced by oversimplified conceptual schemes contradicted by experience. The more difficult it is to use the prevailing conceptual scheme to make sense of experience, the more the social situation will be thrown into confusion and left to ad hoc negotiations. Negotiations provide the opportunity for persons to elude labeling when otherwise these persons might be sanctioned. Black and white categories about deviance may at times serve to discourage behavior which risks labeling by exaggerating the horrors of crossing the line from good to bad. But when the categories are undermined, risky behavior may flourish. And the more simple any system of categories, the more likely it is to be undermined by the complexity of events (p. 222). (Italics added)

If we accept her interpretation, it is clear that the lesbian woman can have a great deal of influence in the negotiation process by determining how much and what kinds of risky behavior to engage in and/or by aiding in the process of defining a situation as "nothing unusual is happening." Emerson suggests eight factors which may force noncompliance with the easier "nothing unusual is happening" stance. She feels that 1) overwhelming emotion, 2) complexity of performance required if "nothing unusual" stance is taken, 3) degree of certainty that "something unusual is happening," 4) commitment to upholding rules violated, 5) experience with imposing "something unusual is happening" in similar situations, 6) unfavorable disposition toward the deviant, 7) higher the status differential between nondeviant and deviant, and 8) the less drastic the action required by the stance that "something unusual is happening" all may push toward the "something unusual" definition of the situation. Finally, the work of Glaser and Strauss (1964) describes the negotiation of awareness contexts, and they point out that a change in identity of one interactant in the eyes of the other can force a change in awareness context. Although they talk more about the awareness context itself, it is clear from their descriptions of various contexts vis-a-vis dying patients that different contexts and changes in context will require different behaviors on the part of the interactants.

Labeling and Management as Process

What emerges from the literature is a definition of labeling as a potentially negotiable, flexible, ongoing process, often situational, which is dependent on both the behaviors of the interactants and their interpretations of their own and each other's behaviors, states of awareness, and stance. The data in this study are amenable to an interpretation which fits this conception of deviance management as process. Further, they suggest some refinements in the conception. First, the data have shown that the respondents on the whole react differently in different situational contexts. They have most difficulty and least freedom (visibility issues aside) in those situations and with those individuals where negotiation is most likely to be necessary and where 1) the appearance of "nothing unusual is happening" is costly or difficult to maintain, and 2) the interpretation of "something unusual is happening" would be likely to evoke negative sanctions. Situations involving relatives, close friends, and work associates all fall into these two areas; straight parties are also easily located here. Relatives and straight friends are likely to find, at least initially, that the conception of someone loved as deviant is sufficiently threatening to be considered as "something unusual." Emerson (p. 221) points out that, for normals in respect of the deviance in question, "'a deviant could not possibly be a person like . . . me' is an underlying assumption: on the contrary, the deviant is a monster with whom (I) have nothing in common and who is so grotesque as to be incomprehensible to (me)." She states further that, in order to reconcile the discrepancy between deviant as monster and deviant as someone known, people can respond in one of the following ways:

1. the actor is a monster;
2. the 'deviant is a monster' assumption is not correct;
3. the actor is not deviant;
4. the actor is deviant, but the case is an exception to the 'deviant as monster' assumption.

Emerson feels that responses 3 and 4 cause the least social disruption and thus have the lowest cost. On these grounds, she feels they are most likely to be chosen if these conditions are not overridden by the circumstances listed above. What the deviant individual must risk is that the individual to whom she reveals herself will not agree to negotiate toward a "nothing unusual is happening" stance. This type of framework helps to make sense of a number of findings. First, it illuminates the difficulty respondents reported at straight parties and at restaurants. Both of these are situations in which it would undoubtedly be more difficult to sustain the "nothing unusual" stance than in other situations listed. The more visible the individual feels she is, the more likely others are to find her and/or her behavior unusual and sanctionable. Furthermore, these are both extremely public situations. At a party and at a restaurant, as long as one remains in the situation, one is in the public eye. One is thus required to be continually negotiating interpretations. Even though, for example in the restaurant, one may not be actively confronted by negative reactions "it is difficult to forget the outsiders' perspective when one must continually engage in practices which implicitly acknowledge it" (Emerson 1973). The other situations mentioned— having a partner phone at work, going to a movie, asking for a book, or asking for a double bed in a motel—all require some encountering of the public in the form of the business agent involved. All, however, allow the individual reasonably immediate escape from negotiation. Once the book is purchased, the motel room paid for, the movie ticket secured, the actress is free to move once again into a private or semiprivate world in which negotiation is liable to be unnecessary, even though the individual may feel conspicuous. Action is not likely to be taken; the stance that something unusual is happening is unlikely to be invoked. In order to test these assumptions, it would, of course, be desirable to be able to predict beforehand in what situations devi- ants would expect or experience the most difficulty. This is unfor- tunately beyond the scope of this study.

A second piece of data which seems to fit reasonably well into this framework is the difference in freedom to engage in risky be- havior which is found among the various situations. Davis discusses the negotiation of interaction by visible deviants. If we assume that risky behaviors make deviance visible and that visibility of behavior is comparable in consequence to having an unavoidably visible stigma, then we might assume that deviants who, intentionally or unintention- ally, become visible may undergo similar negotiations. Both Davis' "fictional acceptance" and "reciprocal role-taking around a normal- ized projection of self" may be seen as being related to Emerson's "nothing unusual is happening" stance. Each requires in varying degrees intentionally putting the deviance in question into soft focus, pretending that it does not exist. For all intents and purposes, in the situation in which individuals are presumed not to know that another is a lesbian, even though there may be suspicion, nothing unusual is happening, and the matter of deviance need not come into focus at all, at least in an admitted way, for the nondeviant. The lesbian, on the other hand, may, as has been shown, go through a great deal of difficulty with impression management, including the denial or bowd- lerization of large segments of her personal life. It is she who would seem to bear the brunt of maintaining a normal stance with which all concerned can be ostensibly at ease.

Once the deviance is put into sharp focus by being admitted or discussed, negotiations must then be undertaken in a different fashion. In order to maintain the pretense that nothing unusual is happening, it may be necessary for the deviant to aid the nondeviant by not confronting him or her with evidence which would serve to raise uncomfortable questions or which might transform a daughter or close friend from someone who is vaguely connected with practices one doesn't really understand to someone who lives with, is in love with, and makes love with another woman. It is one thing to know in a distant sort of way that someone one has known all one's life is involved with another woman. It is knowledge of a different sort to see her holding hands with, embracing, sharing personal information with, and sleeping with another woman. Thus, to become a stated deviant, to change the awareness context of a relationship from a closed or suspicious to an open one is potentially to be identified as "monster" and to have to negotiate one's way out of a very unpleasant social situation. One possible way of facilitating such negotiations, or even of avoiding the necessity for them altogether, would be to refrain from behavior considered typical or indicative of the label in question. Thus, the lesbian who reduces the cost of continually hiding from loved ones by coming out in the open may also reduce social costs by agreeing (frequently in an unspoken way) to curtail behavior which would throw the "nothing unusual" assumption into doubt. Hence, the situation quoted earlier in which the woman commented that, although her family knew she was lesbian, they would rather talk about it than see direct evidence of it.

Changes in the Lesbian Community

Looking at the pattern of responses across the independent and dependent measures, what is clearest is the extent to which concern about being identified (as contrasted with feeling identifiable) makes a difference in the way respondents say they behave. It seems likely that the increasing prevalence and visibility of the Women's and Gay Liberation movements may be altering the types of stances that lesbian women take and may be altering the way relationships between lesbians and nonlesbians are negotiated. In the gay movement over the last few years, there has been an increasing concern with how to come out of the closet (Cronin 1974; Jay and Young 1975) and a growing sense of identification with the gay subculture, at least on the part of a number of respondents. There seems to be an increasing sense of pride and self-respect and a feeling that being gay is a positive thing. This growing feeling of positive self-regard and increased identification is not, of course, connected unilaterally with coming out. In this sample, for instance, we are not talking about women who have come out completely or who are largely up-front about their sexual preference. Most of the women seem to be somewhere between in and out of the closet: uncomfortable with restrictions; not entirely free to behave with straights as they do with gays; having told some, but by no means all, of the people they know. While most attest to the positive, liberating effects of being lesbian and see it as important in their lives, they also express the negative aspects and feel these strongly. Most also seem to limit socializing to gay friends or straight friends who know they are gay. Life for many of these women does seem to be clearly split between public life, in which they act and appear straight, and their private life, in which they can be more at ease. The public life, which for many includes relationships with relatives, work associates, and straight friends, appears to be the most difficult part to manage. The private lives of these women often sound rich and fulfilling, a fact which is frequently not mentioned in articles on lesbian women. The tragedy, or to be less melodramatic, the unfortunate thing, is that the richness in one area cannot easily be communicated to the other. As one woman wrote:

> (Being lesbian is) fabulous on communication; hell in interfacing with straight society. . . . (I'm) growing much freer but also restricting self-expression with family and work associates when (I) thought originally (I) would be more 'up-front.'

And another woman commented:

> After spending forty hours a week with strait (sic) women and feeling that I am in a strait jacket I prefer spending the rest of my time with lesbian women. Spending time with other gay women is important because I can be myself. . . . Having to act as though I am straight at work is the negative aspect to being a gay woman.

And a third woman said:

> Sometimes (being gay) limits my life, but that is primarily a choice for me as I'd generally prefer to be with lesbian women than with straight people. Once involved within the lesbian community, life flows very easily—my doubts are that life in such an isolated environment can be restrictive plus my fear that leaving the community I'd have no support.

The dependent variables in Hypothesis ID (p. 26) included behavioral as well as situational measures, and, as with the situational measures, self-perceived visibility increases risk taking while thinking about being identified decreases it. As with the situational measures, no differences were predicted in effects of these three measures, and the differences found cannot be explained by the data. However, the fact that these findings point to the importance of the individual's attitude toward visibility seems to be the most relevant thing.

The women who worry about being identified appear to be those who either pay most attention to maintaining a "nothing unusual" stance, or who are more aware that certain kinds of behavior are liable to cause them to be identified. Garfinkel was quoted earlier as saying that those who pass do so by knowing how to make "appearances of . . . sexuality-as-usual decidable as a matter of course." It seems likely that in most social situations, sexual preference is readily assumed to be heterosexual as a matter of course, and the major management job is to avoid giving information which would challenge this assumption. For the deviant, the closed context may be in some instances far easier than any other to manage. The "texture of relevances" involved, for example, on the job or with relatives, is probably much more subtle than can be picked up by this questionnaire. What must be done is to keep one's private life as separate as possible from one's public life. While this is to a great extent true for people in general, the boundary between public and private may be in a different place for lesbian women than for others. It may also require greater thought and effort to keep the boundaries in place while sustaining a "situation as usual" interpretation, particularly about any relationship in which these boundaries would be expected to be more flexible than the lesbian can afford to have them. The difference here is that the facts of private life which most people are willing to share and which they take for granted in a woman, for example, interest in and/or relationships with men, desire for or participation in marriage and the raising of a family, dating, "feminine" topics, and the like, may not be available to lesbian women as matters of discussion. Their equivalents are not suitable for revelation without calling into question the usualness of the situation. Hence, women in the study reported avoiding discussion of private-life matters except in terms which would allow the interpretation that "nothing is unusual here," such as the use of "I went camping" as opposed to "my roommate and I went camping." It is also obvious that a lesbian woman cannot afford, even though she may be known to be gay, to come to work expressing joy over her lover; cannot share the kinds of stories people are wont to tell about dates, lovers, and mates; cannot express sorrow or pain at the dissolution of a relationship or the loss of a loved one; cannot show excessive concern over a partner's illness or worries.

The more concerned one is over being identifiable as a lesbian, the more it appears one attempts to create a "situation as usual" interpretation, or, perhaps, the more difficulty one has with negotiating such a situation. It should be noted that, once the deviance becomes mentioned, concern about being identified no longer distinguishes those who think about being identified from those who do not. Thus, it is apparently the threat of being discovered which is uncomfortable; once the deviance has been made visible, concern about being identified does not appear to matter.

Sexual Experience and Management

The hypotheses relating to sexual experience and management were not substantiated at all. This is not so surprising after looking at the other data. Social situations requiring management are avoided by these women whenever possible. The one situation in which marriage made a difference was at a straight party, in the event that the married respondent went alone. Other situations difficult for lesbian women—work, with relatives, or with straight friends who don't know the respondent is gay—obviously carry the same threats for the married woman or the woman with heterosexual experience as they do for others in this sample. What this suggests is that past history is not much help for these women in negotiating current situations. Since most of the women in the sample do not feel highly visible in any event, having heterosexual experience apparently does not provide much in the way of added invisibility. The problem is not so much in appearance as it is in managing the interface between public and private life, especially in relationships with friends and family. People do frequently discuss their home lives: vacations, dates, weekends, trips, plans, and the like. To share one's private life to some extent is expected. Even, or perhaps especially, acquaintances met by chance on trains, planes, and buses share the demographic details of one's life. Those who are in a position to see one day-to-day or to intrude into one's life in an in-depth way expect not only to know demographic details but emotional and personal details as well. Unless the focus of even temporary relationships can be kept in the here and now, management of information is liable to become a tricky business. This is apparently a problem that experience with men cannot solve.

Unpredicted, but of great interest for future research in this area, are findings which indicate that the study of lesbianism as a form of social deviance may require the revision of some prevailing notions. Lesbian women like those in this study are in a rapidly changing and frequently complex situation which is different from that of many other social deviants. With the increasing influence of the Women's and Gay Liberation movements, the growing number of gay men and women who are coming out, and the changing attitudes toward lesbianism (although these changes are admittedly slow), being lesbian has taken on new dimensions. For the women in this sample, lesbianism is demonstrably an important and overwhelmingly positive choice of life style, particularly as it relates to the existence of a lesbian community. As these women begin to think of themselves and their sexual preference in a more positive light, the issue of management seems to be changing. Women who are lesbian are now not only struggling with the issues and problems of being considered deviant and thus potentially punishable but also with whether or not, where, when, and with whom to come out:

> I have a hunch that my need for concealment of my gay-
> ness out of fear of rejection and nonacceptance is over-
> determined, but at this point I'm afraid to test reality.
> I'm gradually becoming a little looser about not hiding
> and pretending. One of the biggest crises in my life that
> I can imagine would be dealing with the consequences of
> making and acting on the decision to be totally open
> about my gayness.

Furthermore, as the life style becomes more acceptable to these women, more legitimized, and more publicized, these women come to feel more positively about themselves:

> The importance (of being lesbian) to me is my accept-
> ance of myself—this is fairly recent—last 5 years—
> so I am still learning and growing in what I consider
> to be a pretty healthy personal place. It's still impor-
> tant in that sense, but on another level—it's irrelevant—
> it's become so as I have come to accept myself—I don't
> think about it as I relate more openly and with less fear
> and guilt with colleagues and students. Many faculty
> and students are aware of my life style and it's cool.
> The less uptight I get, the less I think about it—but
> the more I enjoy myself and my lovers.

With this growing sense of positive self-awareness comes an increasing intolerance for restrictions:

> I have changed a lot. Five years ago I was ending a
> marriage of 12 years and just beginning through the
> women's movement and my lesbian lover to become

myself. I have become radical and have much less
patience with restrictions.

One or two years ago I wasn't sure I wanted to be gay
or really was happy. I'm becoming more intolerant of
restrictions on being gay. I would like to be socially
accepted universally. I'm tired of hiding my feelings
and feeling 'shut up.' I have changed because I feel
more at ease with myself. I no longer feel I'm doing
something wrong.

I am freer in my life style and less willing to accept
restrictions of gay life than I was five years ago. I
feel this change in attitude is primarily due to moving
to California, to the changing role of women, and to
society's greater acceptance of deviations from the
'norm.'

Management is a problem for these women, certainly, but it
is a rather different proposition from what was expected. Both
writers about lesbians (for example, Aldrich; Cory) and sociologists
writing about deviance (for example, Becker; Garfinkel; Goffman)
have focused largely on the problems of being deviant. This led the
author to view lesbianism as an experience much more difficult and
problematic than it actually appears to be for this sample of women.
While the respondents certainly do report some instances in which
being lesbian presents problems, there is not a great sense of trauma
about it. For some, indeed, the problems are seen as being no different from, or even less than, those of being straight:

I really don't see any negative aspects to being a gay
woman that are any different from what straight people
experience in their relationships—old age, death, and
so on are universal problems I feel. . . .

I think of it as a very difficult life to live (because it
is neither accepted nor condoned) but far better than
living the traditional female role with all its humilia-
tions.

I feel free now, and I felt I had to manage my life more
when I was trying to be heterosexual and fitting into a
role that was not natural for me.

(Being lesbian is) pretty important . . . and a large
part of my life. I hated relating to men sexually and

> emotionally. I felt so oppressed, but it took me a long
> time for me to get the strength to get out of the passive
> traditional role. Being part of the gay subculture has
> legitimatized (sic) me to be strong and free and I don't
> see how one can do that in a straight 'world.' So with-
> out the gay subculture I'd be pretty lost.

While these women do express dissatisfaction with the problems and
while they do report negative consequences to their life style, there
is little of the sense of oppression and misery which runs through
much of the writing about lesbian women (particularly the more dated
writing). The tortured searchings and painful sensitivity of Radclyffe
Hall's Stephen in Well of Loneliness, the pathetic, sometimes furtive,
highly sensationalized exposés of Cory's and Aldrich's women, the
heavy-handed sense of being misunderstood and neurotic that pervades
these works—these are simply not characteristic of the women in this
sample. They are not miserable and desperate; they are not consumed
by their deviance; they do not bemoan their fate. Some are angry,
few are entirely satisfied, but most of these women feel that being
lesbian is their choice and that the choice is a good one, for all its
inevitable difficulties. The overall impression received from these
women is probably best summed up by a quote from one woman who
said:

> This questionnaire really focuses on the negative aspects
> (of being a lesbian). I think being gay is wonderful and
> the problems are fewer than when I was straight, al-
> though very different. Please don't focus your study
> on the problem/restrictions—remember the joy and
> love and happiness. . . . I have more meaningful and
> deep relationships with friends now. I have more
> friends. I have a sense of community and a cause.
> I have a more open and joyous lover/friend relation-
> ship. Being gay is a learning process as well as a
> life style. My life is worth living now. I can be an
> individual now. I'm actually very open with being gay.
> The problems are there, but they aren't my major
> concern. (Italics added)

This attitude, and it is not unique to this one respondent, is one which
has not been studied or presented as representative of any type of
behavior and/or life style considered socially deviant. For these
women and their gay sisters, the conception of management seems
to be changing: the focus is less on meshing with the straight culture
than on living as well as possible within one's own frame, and the
most difficult management problems may increasingly be not how to

live as a hidden deviant but how to live as someone who has come out.
Ultimately, for both gay and straight individuals, this may mean a
revising of concepts and expectations. These women do not take an
apologetic stance. While they are in general careful not to inflict
their sexual preference on straight people (that is, they don't feel
the same freedom of behavior with such individuals as with other gay
people), they do not at all fit the stereotype of "the love that dare
not speak its name." This new and positive consciousness would
seem to require reconsideration of the issues of management. Lesbian women will undoubtedly be considered deviant by much of society
for a long time to come. Even in coming out they do not really fit
the definition of the visible deviant for their deviance is primarily
behavioral (unless they are in drag), and thus they have the option
of remaining hidden or of putting their lesbianism into soft focus by
not calling attention to it or acting upon it. It is obviously one thing
to say one is lesbian and something else altogether to act like one
in public. The dynamics of this type of negotiation are really only
beginning to be explored as they relate to lesbian women and certainly
have not been significantly studied within the context of the changing
times.

   Also unexamined thus far in the deviance literature is the whole
complex of behaviors and consequences involved in the process of
coming out for the lesbian woman and the straight people involved.
The possibility of coming out and pressure to do so within the gay
community may radically alter the sociology of that community within
the next few years. The final conclusion of this study must be that
the study of lesbianism as a form of socially ostracized behavior
must in the future take into account the changing pressures on and
self-perceptions of women within the lesbian community. This study
points out that the major variable for these women is not visibility
per se but concern about visibility. It was also clear that concern
about visibility has decreased or is decreasing for some of these
women as they become impatient with restrictions on their behavior.
This suggests that management for lesbian women will not only have
to take place to some extent vis-a-vis the straight community but
may begin to be necessary within the lesbian community as well as
women loosen up, become more militant, and thereby threaten and
enrich not only straight society but many within the gay community
itself.

SUMMARY AND CONCLUSIONS

   The findings indicate that the major determinant of management for the women in this sample is the extent to which an individual

is concerned about being identified as a lesbian woman when around straight people. The more a woman worries about being identified, the more difficult she finds a number of situations, the more behaviors she is liable to engage in in order not to be identified as a lesbian woman, and the fewer risk-taking behaviors she will engage in in some situations. Self-perceived visibility is not, however, consistently related to management. The higher the self-perceived visibility, the greater the difficulty in some situations, but the less management is undertaken in others.

Significant differences were found in the numbers of behaviors women thought they would feel free to engage in in various types of situations: with straights (relatives, public, friends) who don't know one is gay; with straights who know one is gay; and with other gay people. Significant differences were also found in types of behaviors women were willing to engage in: the more revealing the behavior, the less likely women were to engage in it.

Heterosexual experience, whether measured by marital experience or by sexual experience with men, made no difference in ease of management except at a straight party where having been married made the situation significantly less difficult. It is felt that this is probably due to two factors: 1) the women in the sample were already reasonably well normalized by appearance and behavior when they chose to be, and 2) the real problem was in dealing with one's current private life, not one's situational behavior, except insofar as that behavior would clearly identify one as a lesbian.

It is believed that the results can be understood by reference to the sociological literature on the negotiation of relationships vis-a-vis a particular form of deviance. There were only a few situations given in which visibility might make the assumption that nothing unusual is happening difficult to maintain. Other situations really require management of visibility through control of information and behavior. Even in those instances in which women are with straights who know they are gay, the stance that nothing unusual is happening is apparently facilitated by the lesbian woman curtailing some behavior which might force the interpretation that something unusual is happening. The fact that higher visibility is associated with greater freedom to engage in risky behavior and that greater concern over being identified is associated with less freedom to engage in risky behavior is viewed in terms of the different situations in which these differences are obtained. It is noted that concern over visibility only makes a difference with individuals who do not know the respondent is gay. Once the deviance can be considered revealed, this variable no longer has an effect.

Finally, the data suggest that the study of deviance management as it applies to lesbian women may need to take into account some new factors. If the women in this sample are in any way representative, identity management for lesbian women in the future may increasingly include the issue of coming out. It is felt that such a change would affect the way in which both lesbians and straights negotiate relationships. Such changes should thus have implications for individual lesbian women, the lesbian community, and the study of the sociology of deviance as it relates to that community.

APPENDIX A:
QUESTIONNAIRE

QUESTIONNAIRE

1. Age:_____

2. Place of birth: _____

3. City where currently living (if outside California, please include state):_____

4. Occupation:_____

5. Education: 1) Some high school ___   6) Post-grad.___
              2) High school graduate___   7) Masters ___
              3) Some college ___   8) Doctorate ___
              4) A.A. ___   9) Post-doc ___
              5) B.A. ___

6. Marital status: 1) Never married ___
                     2) Currently married ___
                     3) Separated ___
                     4) Divorced ___
                     5) Widowed ___

7. Do you have any children? 1) Yes___   2) No___

   If yes, how many children: boys___   girls___

   What are the ages of the youngest and oldest child?
           Youngest _____
           Oldest_____

   Are any of your children living with you now? 1) Yes___
                                                  2) No___

8. Do you currently have a lover or partner (female)?
           1) Yes___
           2) No ___

9. If you do have a lover or partner, how long have you been involved?
   1) Less than 1 month ___
   2) Between 1 and 6 months ___
   3) 6 months to a year ___
   4) More than 1 but less than 5 years ___
   5) 5 years or more ___
   6) Not applicable ___

10. How many relationships have you had with women which have lasted longer than 6 months (include current relationship if applicable)?
1) One such relationship___
2) 2 such relationships ___
3) 3 such relationships ___
4) 4 such relationships ___
5) 5 or more such relationships___

11. If you <u>do</u> currently have a lover or partner, are you living together?
1) Yes___   2) No___   3) Not applicable ___

12. If you do not currently have a lover or partner, have you ever lived with another woman in a partnership or love relationship?
1) Yes___   2) No___   3) Not applicable___

13. What is the longest period of time you have lived with another woman in a lover or partner relationship?
0) Have never lived with another woman in such a relationship   ___
1) Longest time 1 year or less   ___
2) Longest time between 1 and 5 years   ___
3) Longest time more than 5 but less than 10 years   ___
4) Longest time 10 years or more   ___

14. What is the longest period of time you have been involved with another woman in a lover or partner relationship?
0) Have never been involved with another woman   ___
1) Longest time 1 year or less   ___
2) Longest time between 1 and 5 years   ___
3) Longest time more than 5 but less than 10 years   ___
4) Longest time 10 years or more   ___

15. Using the Kinsey scale given below, please rate yourself on the basis of your sexual history. Circle the number which most closely describes your experience.
0—Entirely heterosexual
1—Largely heterosexual but with incidental homosexual history
2—Largely heterosexual but with distinct homosexual history
3—Equally heterosexual and homosexual
4—Largely homosexual but with a distinct heterosexual history

5—Largely homosexual but with incidental heterosexual history
6—Entirely homosexual
X—Without either

16. Which of the following individuals do you think know that you are gay?
Mother or female guardian ___
Father or male guardian ___
Brother(s) ___
Sister(s) ___
Other relatives ___
Most people at work or school situation ___
Some men in your work or school situation ___
Some women in your work or school situation ___
Almost all of the people you know ___
Best heterosexual friend of the same sex ___
Most other heterosexual friends of same sex ___
Best heterosexual friend of the opposite sex ___
Most of your neighbors ___

17. How many of the above are you certain know you are gay because you have told them or have talked about it with them? Please underline those individuals in the list above who you are sure know that you are gay.

18. How much contact do you have with straight people in your work situation?
1) Work with predominantly straight people ___
2) Work with about half straight, half gay people ___
3) Work with predominantly gay people ___
4) Work with all gay people ___
5) Work with all straight people except myself ___
6) Not applicable ___

19. How much contact do you have with straight people in social situations? See straight people socially at least:
1) Twice a week ___
2) Once a week ___
3) Twice a month ___
4) Once a month ___
5) Less often than once a month ___

20. Do you consider yourself a feminist? 1) Yes___   2) No___

21. Have you participated in any women's groups, e.g. consciousness-raising or feminist groups?
    1) Yes___   2) No___

22. Have you participated in any gay rap groups or consciousness-raising groups?   1) Yes___   2) No___

23. Do you belong to any women's rights or political groups, e.g. NOW, NWPC, or other local groups?
    1) Yes___   2) No___

24. Do you belong to any groups designed to further the cause of gay people, e.g. Gay Liberation, local gay speaker's bureau, etc.?   1) Yes___   2) No___

25. Have you read or are you reading any of the following?
    Lesbian/Woman   ___
    Sappho Was a Right-On Woman ___
    Rubyfruit Jungle   ___
    Lesbian Nation   ___
    Out of the Closet: Voices from Gay Liberation ___
    Other books about gay women or gay liberation ___
    Other literature (articles, magazines, etc.)
       about gay women or gay liberation   ___

26. Do you subscribe to or read regularly any magazines or newspapers published by and for the gay community?
    1) Yes___   2) No___

27. How much contact do you have with other gay women (besides your partner)?
    See other gay women socially at least:
    1) Twice a week   ___
    2) Once a week   ___
    3) Twice a month   ___
    4) Once a month   ___
    5) Less often than once a month ___

28. How often do you go to gay bars?
    Go to a gay bar at least:
    1) Twice a week   ___
    2) Once a week   ___
    3) Twice a month   ___
    4) Once a month   ___
    5) Once every 6 months   ___

6) Once every year ___
7) Less often than once a year ___

29. Do you think straight people can tell that you're gay?
    Almost always___   Often___   Sometimes___
    Seldom___   Never___

30. When you are around straight people, how often do you think
    about whether they will know you're gay?
    Almost always___   Often___   Sometimes___
    Seldom___   Never___

31. When you are with your partner or another gay woman in
    (straight) public places or in the company of straight people,
    do you think you are more likely to be identified as a gay
    woman than when you are alone?
    Almost always___   Often___   Sometimes___
    Seldom___   Never___

32. When and if you are in situations where you think people might
    identify you as a gay woman, what do you think might cause
    them to so identify you? Check as many as apply to you.
    Walk   ___   Body build
    Hair style   ___   Single status   ___
    Reaction to women___   Interests   ___
    Reaction to men   ___   Occupation   ___
    Stance   ___   Lack of "feminine"
    Way of sitting   ___   characteristics   ___
    Way of talking   ___   Too many "masculine"
                                      characteristics   ___
                                   Other_____
                                   _____

33. Do you like being a gay woman?
    Almost always___   Often___   Sometimes___
    Seldom___   Never___

34. Do you feel that being a lesbian is a definite choice on your
    part or is it something you can't help?
    Entirely my choice   ___
    Mostly my choice   ___
    Partly my choice   ___
    Very little my choice   ___
    Not my choice at all   ___

95

35. Please rate the following situations according to the degree to which they make you feel awkward or uncomfortable because you are a gay woman. Use the numbers below to indicate degree of difficulty of each situation.
1 = Extremely difficult; 2 = Quite difficult; 3 = Somewhat difficult; 4 = Slightly difficult; 5 = Not at all difficult; X = Not applicable

1) Going out in public with a group of women _____
2) Getting a motel room for yourself and your partner _____
3) Getting a motel room with a double bed for yourself and your partner _____
4) Going to a straight party alone _____
5) Going to a straight party with your partner _____
6) Going alone to a movie which depicts a lesbian woman or women _____
7) Going to such a movie with another gay woman _____
8) Buying a book about lesbians or lesbianism _____
9) Going to a nice restaurant with your partner _____
10) Going repeatedly to the same restaurant, store, etc. with your partner _____
11) Having your partner pick you up at work or school _____
12) Having your partner phone you frequently at work _____
13) Going to a concert, play, opera, etc. with your partner _____
14) Having straight friends to your home _____
15) Having relatives to your home _____

36. Please circle the numbers of any of the above situations which you regularly avoid because of being a gay woman.

37. If there are any other situations which you find difficult or try to avoid, please describe them in the space below.

38. For each situation presented below, please indicate in the space provided which of the following behaviors you and your partner would generally feel free to engage in. For example, if you usually feel free to show both physical and verbal affection when with relatives but do not feel free to do any of the other things, you would place a (1) and a (2) on the line below item A.
1) Feel free to show physical affection
2) Feel free to show verbal affection
3) Feel free to use nicknames, terms of endearment, etc.
4) Feel free to discuss your relationship

96

5) Feel free to interact on a "personal" level, e.g., argue, discuss financial matters, future plans; in other words, feel free to interact as lovers or partners, as a couple

6) Feel free to use pronouns such as "we," "our," or "ours" when discussing decisions, experiences, jointly owned property, etc.

7) Feel free to be in close physical proximity, e.g., sit next to each other, stand close together, move around together, etc.

A. If you and your partner have ever gone together to visit your relatives, which of the above items apply to the way you behaved?

_____

B. If your partner has ever visited you at work or at school or been with you in the company of associates from work or school, list the items which apply to those situations.

_____

C. When you and your partner are in "straight" public, list as many of the items from above as generally apply to your behavior.

_____

D. If you and your partner ever visit or are visited by straight friends who do not know or have never acknowledged the fact that you're gay, how many of the items above apply to your behavior?

_____

E. If you and your partner ever visit or are visited by straight friends who do know that you're gay, please list above items which apply.

_____

F. If you and your partner ever go to a gay bar or gay party, please list the items which apply.

_____

G. Which of the items apply when you are with your closest gay friends?

_____

39. Have you ever felt that it was necessary to disguise your life style in any of the following ways in order to hide the fact that you are a lesbian?
1) Using the pronoun "he" instead of "she" to refer to a roommate or lover   ___

2) Pretending to be engaged   ___
3) Actually getting engaged   ___
4) Pretending to be married   ___
5) Actually getting married   ___
6) Pretending to date men   ___
7) Actually dating in order to keep up appearances   ___
8) Inviting a gay man as your "date" to social functions   ___
9) Lying about your living situation   ___
10) Avoiding talking about your living situation   ___
11) Avoiding being seen in public places with gay friends   ___
12) Pretending not to see or recognize a gay friend
    when with straight people   ___
13) Pretending not to see or recognize a straight
    friend when with gay people   ___
14) Introducing your lover or partner as a "friend"   ___
15) Failing to introduce your lover or partner to a
    straight friend when it would have been appropriate
    to do so   ___
16) Other_____
    _____
    _____

40. Which of the following do you feel are advantages to having
    relationships with women rather than men? Use the 5-point
    scale provided to indicate the importance of each item to you.
    1 = Very important, 2 = Quite important, 3 = Somewhat impor-
    tant, 4 = Not too important, 5 = Not at all

    A. Shared responsibility for traditionally feminine tasks   ___
    B. Shared responsibility for traditionally masculine tasks___
    C. Better communication with a woman than with a man   ___
    D. More emotional support from partner   ___
    E. Greater flexibility in role expectations   ___
    F. Freedom from male dominance   ___
    G. Freedom from traditional woman's role   ___
    H. Greater acceptance of traditionally nonfeminine
       behavior   ___
    I. Greater sexual compatibility   ___
    J. Other _____
       _____
       _____

The remaining questions are open-ended. You are encouraged to
write as much as you can in answer to these questions. Please try
to be as specific as possible in giving your answers.

41. In your day-to-day life, are there any social situations which occur frequently which require management on your part to hide the fact that you are gay? If so, please describe these situations and how you hide the fact that you are a lesbian.

42. In your own experience, what are the most positive aspects to being a gay woman?

43. What are the most negative aspects to being a gay woman, in your experience?

44. How important is it to you that you are gay? Is it a large part of your life or a small part, is it very important or largely irrelevant? What makes it so?

45. Is being a gay woman depressing, happy, indifferent, unpleasant? What kind of experience is it and has it been for you to be gay?

46. Does being a gay woman require a great deal of management on your part? Do you find that it is something that you are often concerned about? Does it limit your life in any way? If so, please describe some of the difficulties, concerns, limitations.

47. What is the single most difficult situation or circumstance you have been in which was (or is) due to being gay?

48. How do you think you might have answered this questionnaire 5 or 10 (or even just 1 or 2) years ago? Do you think you have changed as far as the restrictions you are willing to accept? If so, in what ways? If you think you have changed, why do you think you have changed?

49. Do you have anything to add? Please do so here.

APPENDIX B:
DATA TABLES

TABLE B.1

Difficulty in Social Situations

Situation	Mean	Standard Deviation	Variance
Having relatives to home	3.45	1.37	1.87
Going to a straight party with partner	3.45	1.27	1.62
Going to a straight party alone	3.61	1.40	1.95
Asking for double bed in motel	3.81	1.18	1.38
Going alone to a movie depicting a gay woman or women	4.08	1.38	1.91
Having partner phone at work	4.08	1.24	1.54
Going with others to a movie depicting a gay woman or women	4.10	1.13	1.28
Buying a book about gay women	4.23	1.07	1.15
Getting a motel room for self and partner	4.30	1.03	1.05
Having straight friends to home	4.31	.85	.72
Having partner pick you up at work or school	4.58	.74	.54
Going out with a group of gay women	4.62	.79	.63
Going repeatedly to a restaurant with partner	4.62	.77	.59
Going out to a nice restaurant	4.66	.68	.47
Going to a concert or play with partner	4.86	.45	.20

Source: Compiled by the author.

TABLE B.2

Behaviors Respondents Felt Free to Engage in
with Relatives

Behavior	N	Percent
Be in close physical proximity to partner	30	37
Use joint pronouns such as "we," "our"	29	36
Interact as lovers or partners	20	25
Show verbal affection	15	18
Use nicknames, terms of endearment	13	16
Discuss relationship	10	12
Show physical affection	8	10

Source: Compiled by the author.

TABLE B.3

Behaviors Respondents Felt Free to Engage in
at Work or School

Behavior	N	Percent
Be in close physical proximity to partner	30	37
Use joint pronouns such as "we," "our"	23	28
Show verbal affection	17	21
Use nicknames, terms of endearment	15	18
Interact as lovers or as a couple	12	15
Show physical affection	12	15
Discuss relationship	9	11

Source: Compiled by the author.

TABLE B.4

Behaviors Respondents Felt Free to Engage in
in Straight Public

Behavior	N	Percent
Be in close physical proximity to partner	31	38
Use joint pronouns such as "we," "our"	29	36
Show verbal affection	19	24
Use nicknames, terms of endearment	17	21
Interact as lovers or as a couple	16	20
Show physical affection	12	15
Discuss relationship	10	12

Source: Compiled by the author.

TABLE B.5

Behaviors Respondents Felt Free to Engage in
with Straight Friends Who Don't Know Respondent
Is Gay

Behavior	N	Percent
Be in close physical proximity to partner	31	38
Use joint pronouns such as "we," "our"	29	36
Show verbal affection	19	24
Use nicknames, terms of endearment	17	21
Interact as lovers or as a couple	16	20
Show physical affection	12	15
Discuss relationship	10	12

Source: Compiled by the author.

TABLE B.6

Behaviors Respondents Felt Free to Engage in
with Straight Friends Who Know Respondent Is Gay

Behavior	N	Percent
Be in close physical proximity	72	89
Show verbal affection	71	88
Use joint pronouns such as "we," "our"	70	86
Use nicknames, terms of endearment	66	82
Show physical affection	65	80
Discuss the relationship	65	80
Interact as lovers or as a couple	62	76

Source: Compiled by the author.

TABLE B.7

Behaviors Respondents Felt Free to Engage in
at a Gay Bar or Party

Behavior	N	Percent
Be in close physical proximity	72	89
Show verbal affection	71	88
Use joint pronouns such as "we," "our"	70	86
Use nicknames, terms of endearment	66	82
Show physical affection	65	80
Discuss relationship	65	80
Interact as lovers or as a couple	62	76

Source: Compiled by the author.

TABLE B.8

Behaviors Respondents Felt Free to Engage in
with Closest Gay Friends

Behavior	N	Percent
Be in close physical proximity	76	94
Show verbal affection	73	90
Use joint pronouns such as "we," "our"	72	89
Show physical affection	72	89
Use nicknames, terms of endearment	68	84
Interact as lovers or as a couple	68	84
Discuss relationship	66	82

Source: Compiled by the author.

TABLE B.9

Behaviors Engaged in to Avoid
Being Identified as Lesbian

Behavior	N	Percent
Introduce lover or partner as a "friend"	62	76
Avoid talking about living situation	54	67
Pretend to date a man	32	40
Use "he" instead of "she" to refer to lover or partner	27	33
Lie about living situation	23	28
Actually date a man	22	27
Invite a gay man as a "date" to social functions	21	26
Avoid being seen with gay friends	13	16
Pretend not to see a gay friend when with straight people	9	11
Pretend not to see a straight friend when with gay people	9	11
Actually get married	4	5
Get engaged	3	4
Pretend to be engaged	1	1
Pretend to be married	1	1

Mean number of behaviors engaged in = 3.64
S.D. = 2.08
Variance = 4.33
Source: Compiled by the author.

TABLE B.10

Individuals Whom Respondents Think
Know They Are Gay

Individual	N	Percent
Some women at work or school	21	26
Mother or female guardian	15	18
Some men at work or school	14	17
Most neighbors	14	17
Siblings	13	16
Other relatives	13	16
Almost all of the people you know	9	11
Father or male guardian	8	10
Most people at work or school	8	10
Best heterosexual friend—female	5	6
Best heterosexual friend—male	5	6
Children	5	6
Most heterosexual friends—male	4	5
Most heterosexual friends—female	3	4

Mean = 2.19
S.D. = 3.15
Variance = 9.92
Source: Compiled by the author.

TABLE B.11

Individuals Whom Respondents Are Sure
Know They Are Gay

Individual	N	Percent
Best heterosexual friend—female	45	56
Siblings	35	43
Best heterosexual friend—male	31	38
Some women at work or school	30	37
Mother or female guardian	30	37
Most heterosexual friends—female	27	33
Father or male guardian	20	25
Most heterosexual friends—male	20	25
Some men at work or school	19	23
Almost all of the people you know	16	20
Most people at work or school	11	14
Other relatives	8	10
Most neighbors	6	7
Children	4	5

Mean = 3.54
S.D. = 3.25
Variance = 10.54
Source: Compiled by the author.

BIBLIOGRAPHY

Abbott, Sidney, and Love, Barbara. 1972. Sappho Was a Right-On Woman. New York: Stein and Day.

Akers, Ronald L. 1968. "Problems of Definition and Behavior in the Sociology of Deviance." Social Forces 46:455-65.

Aldrich, A. 1963. We Two Won't Last. Greenwich, Conn.: Fawcett Publications.

____. 1958. We, Too, Must Love. New York: Fawcett Publications.

____. 1955. We Walk Alone. New York: Fawcett Publications.

Altman, Dennis. 1971. Homosexuals: Oppression and Liberation. New York: Avon Books.

Armon, Virginia. 1960. "Some Personality Variables in Overt Female Homosexuality." Journal of Projective Techniques 24: 292-99.

Ashworth, A. E., and Walker, W. M. 1972. "Social Structure and Homosexuality: A Theoretical Appraisal." British Journal of Sociology 23(1):146-58.

Babbie, Earl R. 1975. The Practice of Social Research. Belmont, Calif.: Wadsworth.

Becker, Howard S. 1963. Outsiders: Studies in the Sociology of Deviance. New York: Free Press.

Bergler, Edward. 1957. Homosexuality: Disease or Way of Life. New York: Hill and Wang.

Bieber, Irving. 1976. "A Discussion of 'Homosexuality: The Ethical Challenge.'" Journal of Consulting and Clinical Psychology 44(2):163-66.

Bieber, Irving, et al. 1962. Homosexuality: A Psychoanalytic Study of Female Homosexuals. New York: Basic Books.

Boggan, E. Carrington, et al. 1977. The Rights of Gay People: The Basic ACLU Guide to a Gay Person's Rights. New York: Avon Books.

Caprio, Frank S. 1954. Female Homosexuality: A Modern Study of Lesbianism. New York: Grove Press.

Clark, Donald H. 1977. Loving Someone Gay. Milbrae, Calif.: Celestial Arts.

Cory, Donald W. 1965. The Lesbian in America. New York: Macfadden-Bartell.

Cronin, D. M. 1974. "Coming Out among Lesbians." In Sexual Deviance and Sexual Deviants, ed. Erich Goode and Richard Troiden, pp. 268-77. New York: William Morrow.

Davis, Fred. 1961. "Deviance Disavowal: The Management of Strained Interaction by the Visibly Handicapped." Social Problems 9: 120-32.

Davison, Gerald C. 1976. "Homosexuality: The Ethical Challenge." Journal of Consulting and Clinical Psychology 44(2): 157-62.

Deutsch, Helene. 1933. "Homosexuality in Women." International Journal of Psychoanalysis 14: 34-56.

Dinitz, Simon, Dynes, Russel R., and Clarke, Alfred C. 1969. "Deviance, Norms, and Societal Reactions." In Deviance: Studies in the Process of Stigmatization and Social Reaction, eds. Simon Dinitz, et al., pp. 3-22. New York: Oxford University Press.

Douglas, Jack D. 1972. "Observing Deviance." In Research on Deviance, ed. Jack D. Douglas, pp. 3-34. New York: Random House.

_____. 1966. "Conceptions of Deviant Behavior: The Old and the New." Pacific Sociological Review 9: 9-14.

Douvan, Elizabeth. 1970. "New Sources of Conflict in Females at Adolescence and Early Adulthood." In Feminine Personality and Conflict, pp. 31-44. Belmont, Calif.: Brooks/Cole.

Emerson, Joan P. 1973. "Nothing Unusual Is Happening." In Human Nature and Collective Behavior, ed. Tamotsu Shibutani, pp. 193-207. New Brunswick, N.J.: Transaction Books.

Erikson, Kait. 1968. "Patient Role and Social Uncertainty." In Deviance: The Interactionist Perspective, eds. Earl Rubington and Martin Weinberg, pp. 337-42. London: Macmillan.

____. 1962. "Notes on the Sociology of Deviance." Social Problems 9:307-14.

Freud, Sigmund. 1924. Collected Papers, Volume I. New York: The International Psycho-Analytical Press.

Gagnon, John H., and Simon, W. 1973a. Sexual Conduct: The Social Sources of Human Sexuality. Chicago: Aldine.

Gagnon, John H., and Simon, William, eds. 1973b. The Sexual Scene. New Brunswick, N.J.: Transaction Books.

____. 1967. Sexual Deviance. New York: Harper.

Galana, Lana, and Covina, Gina. 1977. The New Lesbians. Berkeley, Calif.: Moon Books.

Garfinkel, Harold. 1967. Studies in Ethnomethodology. Englewood Cliffs, N.J.: Prentice-Hall.

Giallombardo, Rose. 1966. A Study of a Women's Prison. New York: Wiley.

Gibbs, Jack P. 1972. "Issues in Defining Deviant Behavior." In Theoretical Perspectives on Deviance, eds. Robert A. Scott and Jack D. Douglas, pp. 39-68. New York: Basic Books.

Glaser, Barney G., and Strauss, Anselm L. 1964. "Awareness Contexts and Social Interaction." American Sociological Review 29(5):669-79.

Gnepp, E. H. 1975. "Biology, Mental Illness, and Homosexuality." Psychology 12(4):60-61.

Goffman, Erving. 1974. Frame Analysis: An Essay on the Organization of Experience. New York: Harper.

_____. 1971. <u>Relations in Public</u>. New York: Harper.

_____. 1967. <u>Interaction Ritual: Essays on Face-to-Face Behavior</u>. Garden City, N.Y.: Anchor Books.

_____. 1963. <u>Stigma: Notes on the Management of Spoiled Identity</u>. Englewood Cliffs, N.J.: Prentice-Hall.

Gonsiorek, J. C. 1977. "Psychological Adjustment and Homosexuality." MS. 1478. Abstracted in Journal Supplement Abstract Services (JSAS) <u>Catalog of Selected Documents in Psychology</u> 7(2): 45.

ν Goode, Erich, and Troiden, Richard, eds. 1974. <u>Sexual Deviance and Sexual Deviants</u>. New York: William Morrow.

Gundlach, Ralph H., and Riess, Bernard. 1968. "Self and Sexual Identity in the Female: A Study of Female Homosexuals." In <u>New Directions in Mental Health</u>, Volume I, ed. Bernard F. Riess, pp. 205-31. New York: Grune and Stratton.

_____. 1967. "Birth Order and Sex of Siblings in a Sample of Lesbians and Non-Lesbians." <u>Psychological Reports</u> 20:61-62.

Hadden, S. B. 1976. "Homosexuality: Its Questioned Classification." <u>Psychiatric Annals</u> 6(4):60-61.

Hall, Radclyffe. 1950. <u>The Well of Loneliness</u>. New York: Pocket Books.

Halleck, Seymour L. 1976. "Another Response to 'Homosexuality: The Ethical Challenge.'" <u>Journal of Consulting and Clinical Psychology</u> 44(2):167-70.

Heidensohn, Frances. 1968. "The Deviance of Women: A Critique and an Enquiry." <u>British Journal of Sociology</u> 19(2):160-75.

Hopkins, June H. 1969. "The Lesbian Personality." <u>British Journal of Psychiatry</u> 15:1433-36.

Jay, Karla, and Young, Allen. 1975. <u>After You're Out: Personal Experiences of Gay Men and Lesbian Women</u>. New York: Links Books.

Johnston, Jill. 1973. Lesbian Nation: The Feminist Solution. New York: Simon and Schuster.

Karlen, Arno. 1971. Sexuality and Homosexuality. New York: Norton.

Katz, Jonathan. 1976. Gay American History. New York: Thomas Y. Crowell.

Kaye, Harvey E., et al. 1967. "Homosexuality in Women." Archives of General Psychiatry 17:626-34.

Keiser, Sylvan, and Schaffer, Dora. 1949. "Environmental Factors in Homosexuality in Adolescent Girls." Psychoanalytic Review 36:283-95.

Kenyon, F. E. 1968. "Studies in Female Homosexuality, IV and V." British Journal of Psychiatry 114:1337-50.

Kinsey, Alfred C., et al. 1953. Sexual Behavior in the Human Female. Philadelphia: W. B. Saunders.

Kitsuse, John T. 1962. "Societal Reaction to Deviant Behavior." Social Problems 9:247-56.

Klaich, Dolores. 1974. Woman Plus Woman: Attitudes Toward Lesbianism. New York: Simon and Schuster.

Koedt, Anne. 1974. "Loving Another Woman." In Sexual Deviance and Sexual Deviants, eds. Erich Goode and Richard Troiden, pp. 238-46. New York: William Morrow.

Laing, Ronald D., Phillipson, Herbert, and Lee, A. Russel. 1966. Interpersonal Perception: A Theory and Method of Research. New York: Harper.

Lemert, Edwin M. 1972. Human Deviance: Social Problems and Social Control. Englewood Cliffs, N.J.: Prentice-Hall.

Leznoff, Maurice, and Westley, William A. 1956. "The Homosexual Community." Social Problems 3(4):257-63.

McCaghy, Charles H., and Skipper, James K., Jr. 1973. "Occupational Predispositions and Lesbianism." In Deviance: The Interactionist Perspective, eds. Earl Rubington and Martin S. Weinberg, pp. 260-67. New York: Macmillan.

Mankoff, M. 1971. "Social Reaction and Career Deviance: A Critical Analysis." Sociological Quarterly 12:204-18.

Marmor, Judd. 1974. "'Normal' and 'Deviant' Sexual Behavior." In Sexual Deviance and Sexual Deviants, eds. Erich Goode and Richard Troiden, pp. 45-58. New York: William Morrow.

Martin, Del, and Lyon, Phyllis. 1974. "Lesbian Love and Sexuality." In Sexual Deviance and Sexual Deviants, eds. Erich Goode and Richard Troiden, pp. 238-46. New York: William Morrow.

Martin, Del, and Lyon, Phyllis. 1972. Lesbian Woman. New York: Bantam Books.

Matza, David. 1969. Becoming Deviant. Englewood Cliffs, N.J.: Prentice-Hall.

Meyer, Robert G. 1977. "Legal and Social Ambivalence Regarding Homosexuality." Journal of Homosexuality 2(3):281-87.

Mileski, Maureen, and Black, Donald J. 1972. "The Social Organization of Homosexuality." Urban Life and Culture 1:187-202.

Nie, Norman H. 1975. SPSS: Statistical Package for the Social Sciences. New York: McGraw-Hill.

Plummer, Kenneth. 1975. Sexual Stigma: An Interactionist Account. London: Routledge and Kegan Paul.

Pollack, Stephen T., et al. 1975. "The Dimensions of Stigma: The Social Situation of the Mentally Ill Person and the Male Homosexual." Journal of Abnormal Psychology 85(1):105-12.

Rubington, Earl, and Weinberg, Martin S., eds. 1968. Deviance: The Interactionist Perspective. London: Macmillan.

Sagarin, Edward. 1976. "Thieves, Homosexuals and Other Deviants: The High Personal Cost of Wearing a Label." Psychology Today 9(10):25-31.

Scheff, Thomas J. 1973. "On the Concepts of Identity and Social Relationship." In Human Nature and Collective Behavior, ed. Tamotsu Shibutani, pp. 193-207. New Brunswick, N.J.: Transaction Books.

____. 1967. "Towards a Sociological Model of Concensus." American Sociological Review 32(1):32-46.

____. 1964. "The Societal Reaction to Deviance." Social Problems 11:401-13.

Schofield, Michael G. 1973. Sexual Behavior of Young Adults. London: Penguin Press.

Schur, Edwin M. 1971. Labeling Deviant Behavior. New York: Harper.

Scott, Robert A. 1972. "A Proposed Framework for Analyzing Deviance as a Property of Social Order." In Theoretical Perspectives on Deviance, eds. Robert R. Scott and Jack D. Douglas, pp. 9-35. New York: Basic Books.

Siegelman, Marvin. 1972. "Adjustment of Homosexual and Heterosexual Women." British Journal of Psychiatry 20:477-81.

Simon, William, and Gagnon, John H. 1967a. "Femininity in the Lesbian Community." Social Problems 15(2):212-21.

____. 1967b. "Homosexuality: The Formulation of a Sociological Perspective." Journal of Health and Social Behavior 8:177-85.

____. 1967c. "The Lesbians: A Preliminary Overview." In Sexual Deviance, eds. John H. Gagnon and William Simon, pp. 247-82. New York: Harper.

Simmons, Jerry L. 1969. Deviants. New York: Glendessary Press.

Simpson, Ruth. 1976. From the Closet to the Courts. New York: Penguin.

Taber, Clarence W. 1965. Taber's Cyclopedic Medical Dictionary. 10th ed. Philadelphia: F. A. Davis.

Taylor, Ian, Walton, Paul, and Young, Jack. 1973. The New Criminology. London: Routledge and Kegan Paul.

Thompson, Norman L., Jr., McCandless, Boyd R., and Strickland, Bonnie R. 1971. "Personal Adjustment of Male and Female Homosexuals and Heterosexuals." Journal of Abnormal Psychology 78:237-40.

Ullman, Leonard P., and Krasner, Leonard. 1975. A Psychological Approach to Abnormal Behavior. Englewood Cliffs, N.J.: Prentice-Hall.

Ward, David A., and Kassebaum, Gene G. 1964. "Homosexuality: A Mode of Adaptation for Women in Prison." Social Problems 12:150-77.

Warren, Carol A. B. 1972. "Observing the Gay Community." In Research on Deviance, ed. Jack D. Douglas, pp. 139-64. New York: Random House.

Warren, Carol A. B., and Johnson, John M. 1972. "A Phenomenological Critique of Labeling Theory." In Theoretical Perspectives on Deviance, eds. Robert A. Scott and Jack D. Douglas, pp. 69-92. New York: Basic Books.

Weinberg, George H. 1973. Society and the Healthy Homosexual. Garden City, N.Y.: Anchor Press.

Wilbur, Cornelia B. 1965. "Clinical Aspects of Female Homosexuality." In Sexual Inversion, ed. Judd Marmor, pp. 268-81. New York: Basic Books.

Wilson, Marilyn L., and Greene, Roger L. 1971. "Personality Characteristics of Male and Female Homosexuals." Psychological Reports 28:407-412.

Wysor, Bettie. 1974. The Lesbian Myth. New York: Random House.

ABOUT THE AUTHOR

ALICE MOSES received her M.S.W. and D.S.W. degrees from the University of California, Berkeley. She is now Assistant Professor of Social Work at the University of Tennessee, Knoxville, where she teaches research, social work with groups, and behavior therapy. Dr. Moses also does individual treatment with lesbian clients. She and a fellow social worker are currently writing a book on working with gay clients for those in the helping professions.